Little Miss Akron by Tracey Thomas
First Edition, January 2025
© Tracey Thomas. All rights reserved.

ISBN: 9798304056304
Production Assistance, Cover/Book Design: Ryan Humbert
Editing: Ryan Humbert & Michael Evans

To my tribe, my clan, my family
Scott, Cory, Emma, Marisa, Mara, and Iris

CONTENTS

Foreword *by Ryan Humbert*

Introduction

Chapter One • 1
Little Miss Akron, Little Miss Fairlawn, and Blowing Kisses

"Restless Devil" • 5

Chapter Two • 7
IQ Tests, Billy Dee Williams, a Home of My Own, and the FBI

"Four Seasons" • 17

Chapter Three • 19
Baby, Sometimes Love Just Ain't Enough

"Usually Love" • 23

Chapter Four • 25
Cancer Sun, Scorpio Rising, Libra Moon

"Ghost Town" • 39

Chapter Five • 41
Songs From the Womb

"Yesterday's Child" • 45

Chapter Six • 47
Instability is the New Stability

"Blow Away" • 54

Chapter Seven • 55
My Mother's Keeper

"Oh, Virginia" • 66

Chapter Eight • 68
My Only Sibling and Sitting on the Moon

"Blue Eyes" • 74

Chapter Nine • 76
Tony, What Just Happened?

"Stand Alone" • 82

Chapter Ten • 83
Evolving, Music and Las Vegas

"Ain't I a Woman" • 98

Chapter Eleven • 100
The Akron Sound and Beyond

"Wax on Fire" • 109

Chapter Twelve • 111
The Reason You Bought This Book: Unit 5

"Queen of Nothing" • 118

Chapter Thirteen • 120
More Out-of-Order Ramblings of the Utmost Importance

"Words Can't Save Us Now" • 127

Chapter Fourteen • 129
The Demons We Slay and the Demons That Stay

"Cold" • 138

Chapter Fifteen • 140
Memories of a Wicked Storm

"Wicked Storm" • 145

Chapter Sixteen • 146
My Music Family and Passing it Down

Epilogue • 155

"Space Enough" • 157

"Splinter" • 159

"Hope Flies" • 161

"Traveler on the Wind" • 163

"This World" • 165

Photos • 168

Long Live The Queen • 175
by Bill Gruber

Discography • 178

Bonus Track • 191
by Robert Kidney

FOREWORD

Meeting Tracey Thomas was a fluke. It may never have happened if our lives had moved in slightly different directions, ten minutes earlier or ten minutes later. I'll let Tracey tell the story herself later in the book, but like many "first meetings," total randomness brought us together.

What if I hadn't heard her song "Stand Alone" on the radio while driving through Akron late one night? I loved "Stand Alone" so much that as a thank you to Tracey, I covered it on my first "big-deal" solo album, *Old Souls, New Shoes*, back in 2008. That song started our friendship and will forever be important to me.

All that said, I owe my life in music to Tracey. I'm not sure I'd be writing songs today if it weren't for her. She swears I would, but it's anyone's guess. I'm nearly positive that neither of us has ever co-written more songs with anyone else than we have with one another. To my count, we've penned over twenty songs together, and damn good ones at that. I've learned a lot about songwriting through the process. Like all good friendships and working relationships, she is the yin to my yang. We both bring differing skill sets and talents to the table and truly enjoy helping one another blossom.

We became fast friends after we met over twenty years ago. Over the span of two decades, I've been honored to produce four of her solo albums and her *Best of Tracey Thomas* collection. I was a kid, still in college, when we started working together, and yet she trusted me with her music, art, and gifts. That is not a trust that I take lightly.

Tracey saw something in me that I didn't know existed. She lit that spark and allowed me to figure out how to be a producer and songwriter while allowing me to do so with her songs and career. She gave me the space to do that while being confident in what she wanted. I will always be thankful for that. I'm as proud of those albums as anything I've ever done, and I believe that our newest collaboration, her album *Words Can't Save Us Now*, is the pinnacle of our work together.

As you'll find out while reading *Little Miss Akron*, like all of us, Tracey Thomas is a lot of things: intelligent, hilarious, stubborn, flighty, protective, emotional, loyal, loving, wise, and powerful. She's a nervous, magical free spirit, yet still exhibits calm, strength, and resolve. She's a mystery and an open book. Now, in the most literal sense. She's done it all, for better or worse, and now we all get to share a "piece of her seat." I, for one, can't wait.

Thank you, Tracey, for your trust, friendship, encouragement, and love over the last two decades. You'll always be my favorite *Little Miss Akron*.

Ryan Humbert
North Canton, Ohio
November 2024

Performing "Oh, Virginia" with Ryan Humbert at the Goodyear Theatre in Akron, Ohio, for the Summit FM "330 Day Concert," March 30, 2023

INTRODUCTION

I am a grain of sand on a vast beach. Just one beach on this planet, in this universe, in this reality. My story will probably mean absolutely nothing, in the scheme of things, to anyone but me and mine. And I'm not even sure about mine. I have wondered, "Am I a narcissist for wanting to tell my story? Is it any more interesting than anyone else's?" I went so far as to ask a therapist, who explained that I was not a narcissist and then explained exactly why I would jump to that very self-deprecating conclusion. I think there is a particular "look-at-me" vibe around anyone who chooses a career that puts themself in the spotlight, no matter how small the spotlight may be.

I am a card-carrying member of the PTSD Club, and it isn't easy to deal with any unrest in mind or body. It is even more complex when those disorders are filed under the mental health heading. It has always fascinated me that I crave attention and hate it simultaneously. Being who and how I am, I have difficulty feeling like I deserve any accolades. However, I would lie if I said I didn't adore that attention. I am incredibly sensitive, and even though I have learned to handle constructive criticism, I am easily wounded when it is less than that.

Fortunately, in my music career, I haven't publicly received much criticism, but personal opinions get thrown about with no regard for my well-being. I've had more of the "not-so-constructive" in my personal life and early on in my musical journey. Through the years, I have gotten more savvy at listening, absorbing, taking it in — and throwing it away if needed. That is why I shut the door on career opportunities that came my way. I realized I would be eaten alive in the public eye on a grander scale. I would have ugly cried and turned to drugs, alcohol, and my bed. I've done most of those things just by working the stages here in my hometown of Akron, Ohio. I can't imagine if my career path had been even 100 miles wider, what would have become of me?

I will share stories from my life, early years, family, music career, supernatural dealings, and much more in this book. I won't "Prince Harry" the details (though I love Prince Harry) as my "frostbitten penis" stories are not fit for public consumption.

I sometimes feel the need to explain myself too much. Okay... I always feel the need. I tend to do what I want with a stern reprimand for anyone who questions it, which has not made me the easiest fish to fry (did that work, the fish thing?). I most definitely underestimated its impact on me while crafting this book. I actually didn't remember some of these stories. Friends and family filled me in on wayward memories and reminded me of things I had long forgotten. I am grateful for their input; we had some good laughs and more than a few tears while dredging it all up.

So, welcome to my bubble. I have carefully planted seeds of belief about how life, love, and universes work. Some are based on nothing but faith, some on experience, and many on an extensive exploration of the things we cannot know or define. I believe something unknowable is present and active in my life, which works for me. I am grateful for its presence as I continue to work my life into a meaningful experience.

More often than not, however, I'm usually just pounding square pegs into round holes. You would assume I'd have figured that out by now, but I'm still searching for all the answers, finding cryptic meanings in the most ridiculous things. Like seeing Jesus' face on toast. So here's to discovering yourself, understanding the universe, Jesus, and a good piece of toast.

P.S. Some names have been changed to protect the innocent and to keep me out of court.

ONE:
LITTLE MISS AKRON, LITTLE MISS FAIRLAWN, AND BLOWING KISSES

I have had a life of trauma, instability, and, at times, absolute fear. Early on, I learned to make everything funny. I make people laugh, usually by making myself the brunt of the joke. I don't know why that turned into my "go-to," but it was and still is. I've always thought that if I was laughing, I couldn't simultaneously cry, so I overused that trick.

I was raised by a father who was an alcoholic—one with deep, dark secrets hanging over every aspect of his being. They, in turn, hung over ours. My mother was my rock, but dear God, could she be needy, selfish, and dependent. She also suffered from some mental illnesses, which ended up causing her to be institutionalized at times. I will always believe she had some hormonal issues that were not on the world's radar at the time. Many women's issues weren't, for that matter.

With my mother and father at the helm, I became the poster child for codependency at a very early age. My hellacious need for attention started at the age of three when I began working as a baby model. At the age of six, I was put on the runway, and I did that until I was ten. I was a child model for O'Neill's, an upscale department store based in Northeast Ohio. I would wear the clothes, walk the runway, and get a free lunch in the fancy restaurant beforehand. I always got the chicken pot pie because it came in a "chicken." Not an actual chicken, mind you, but a ceramic dish with a chicken-shaped lid. I was flabbergasted by it. I swear that is why, to this day, I love buying dishware. I buy way too much of it, and it all started with that fantastic chicken pot pie dish at O'Neill's restaurant in Akron, Ohio.

My mom used to tell the story of my first runway gig. It was rather straightforward: I was to walk out, turn around, and walk back. She said they went over the routine with me quite a few times. I would smile, do my walk, spin, and come right back — just like a little blonde, curly-headed pro. On the day of my first paid gig, when the audience was there, I decided to improvise. And so began my long-standing habit of "going off book." I vividly remember walking out and reaching the end of the runway. I felt all the people in the audience loving me so hard. I just stood there and basked in it. My mom said she and the event promoter were calling me, whispering loudly to walk back. I did not. I was digging the love and just stood there, present in the moment. I remembered the "smile" but not the "walk-back" part. Eventually, the event coordinator stomped out and reeled me in to much applause. I was hooked.

I did those shows for years. One year, I modeled an amazing emerald green jumper with a white (or maybe it was yellow?) turtleneck underneath. I loved it so much that they let me keep it. I am sure it was a designer piece because I was a high-end fashionista. I remember being so thrilled that it was mine and excited to wear it to school. Back-to-school fashions were my thing. In some of my class photos, you can see that I was not your average bear. My third or fourth grade class photo shows me in the front, rocking a gold lamé paisley dress — all French and sassy — with a Nehru collar and white go-go boots. My classmates wore plaid skirts, cardigans, and knee socks. My mom had it going on in the fashion department.

Thanks to my illustrious career as a child model, I went on to win the coveted titles of both *Little Miss Akron* AND *Little Miss Fairlawn*. I rode in the back of a convertible, waving to the crowd of onlookers after the Soap Box Derby race, which was always a big deal in Akron. I wore a little glitter sash over my outfit. When I was *Little Miss Akron*, I was around seven or eight. They told me to sit in the car's backseat and, once again, wave and smile. Only this time, I was supposed to blow kisses. Okay, I could do that, being a seasoned model at this point. I took direction well, and people seemed to find me adorable, so I wasn't anxious or nervous.

That day, I was seated with the current *Little Miss Fairlawn*, whose title I would grab soon enough. We were off and running with the politicians, Soap Box Derby champs, and local celebs in a luxurious convertible, cruising through the parade. I remember waving and smiling—and then my lips stuck together when I tried to blow a kiss. I couldn't get them apart. My mouth was so dry, and my lips were really stuck. I nudged *Little Miss Fairlawn*, and she looked at me and laughed. That was it: I was mortified.

I managed to unstick my pucker, but there was bleeding involved, not unlike the scene in *A Christmas Story* with the tongue and the frozen flagpole. Hot summer days, dehydration, wind, and fame make for a bad combination.

I've always remembered that day. I never wanted anyone to laugh at me ever again. It felt horrible. I remember telling my relatives in attendance that my lips got stuck, and they all laughed. My mom didn't, however. She probably drove me to the emergency room because hypochondria is a thing in this tribe, and she was the poster child.

Somewhere, there is a video taken by my favorite Uncle Fred, the husband of my mom's cousin Betty, with an old-school camera. Was it a V8 or something? No, wait—that's tomato juice. Or, as I like to call it, bloody mary mix. Anyway, it was filmed on one of those V8 cameras that were all the rage in the sixties. It exists somewhere: me in the parade, lips stuck together. We used to watch it every year during the holidays, and everyone laughed. My lot in life, I suppose.

As life went on, I had my share of struggles—like everyone—which made the lips-sticking incident seem much less traumatic in the grand scheme of things. I have a pattern of being afraid of being happy. If I ever relax into the feeling that life is too good or predictable, something is bound to slap me in the face. So, I always have my guard up. I work on it to this very day, but that relaxed style of life has always seemed to elude me.

Restless Devil

Written by Tracey Thomas
From the 2020 album *My Roots Are Showing*

Restless devil, why you hold me,
Oh, so tightly, in your grasp?
I'm no angel, but I'm no demon,
Restless devil, let me pass.

Pass through the mountains, through the valley,
That I once knew as my home.
Unencumbered by your tethers,
Free from the darkness of your soul.

I scream "unhand me," but no one's listens,
I'm but a vapor, blowing by.
Put thee behind me, oh blackest nightmare,
So I may see, the morning light.

And when I slay you, oh restless devil,
With my sword of disbelief.
You will be gone, gone forever,
You will not live, you will not breathe.

And God above me, you've let me wander,
From field to ocean, and back again.
I may never know your reason,
'Til I meet you, someday hence.

About Restless Devil: *Not unlike my song "Wax On Fire," "Restless Devil" is pretty autobiographical. I am constantly questioning why I am the way I am. Why am I so like Juliette Binoche's character in the movie Chocolat? I can't settle. I move, shake, and wrestle with anything that has to do with being calm and centered. I know now that, at my age, there is no answer. It's just me being me. This song is about that wondering, that questioning of everything I am.*

TWO:
IQ TESTS, BILLY DEE WILLIAMS, A HOME OF MY OWN, AND THE FBI

Kindergarten, Mrs. Buck, Case Elementary in Akron. Man, was she mean. I remember thinking, "Who is this witch? Is this really who I am supposed to spend half of my day with now?"

Mrs. Buck did not like me. I wasn't too young to jump that train. Admittedly, I was a little hyper—they now call it ADHD, and I am not sure I have ever shaken it from my repertoire. I couldn't concentrate, and she always stood me in the corner. Did she NOT know I was *Little Miss Akron* AND the upcoming upsetter of the current *Little Miss Fairlawn*?

She yelled at me often, banging her ruler on her desk. It was always "Tracey this," and "Tracey that." I never understood why we had to lay on a towel at nap time. I couldn't sleep on a towel. I was used to sleeping in the comfy backseat of our car with my dog Jacques, who was both my white French poodle and my best friend. Living in the car was a luxury compared to this squalor. I hated that floor and the towel and I didn't want to nap. And if I did, not on that hard-ass floor. I'm a big fan of naps now, and I actually have a real bed, so things have improved since kindergarten.

In school, my mind wandered, and it usually wandered to my mother. I was always worried about her. I felt like I had to, or she would disappear. She would fight with my dad, he would be mean, and then she would cry. I felt I was needed at home, and school was a huge interference.

Little Miss Akron

My mother looked like Audrey Hepburn. She was skinny, with black hair and dark brown eyes; she had the "Black Irish" we harbored in our DNA in spades. She wore the most amazing clothes, and people stared at her everywhere she went. My dad was so threatened by everyone who looked at her. It always caused a fight. He was at once so proud to be her guy and yet so insecure because his light wasn't as bright as hers. My dad wasn't gorgeous, but he wasn't ugly. In his youth, he was handsome but looked pretty average once he lost his hair and gained a few pounds. I can absolutely relate.

Mrs. Buck was very short, with grayish blonde hair, tight-curled like the Queen of England, and sensible shoes and clothes. I always thought her shoes were so odd and so ugly, and she wore compression socks with skirts. My mother had a thing for shoes, and her shoes were my favorite thing to put on when I played dress up. I was fascinated by them. They were red, green, silver, some shiny, and some with bows; I still have issues with buying shoes.

I remember being afraid of Mrs. Buck because she looked so different from the people in my tribe, and her shoes scared me. I did not like her, and it was mutual. Of course, there were conferences, but I never cut the mustard with her. In all fairness, I did call her "Mrs. Butts." It's also fair to insert here that karma can be quite the bitch; now, my sister and I both look more like Mrs. Buck than we look like our mom…but I still have badass shoes.

I can only brag up to a point about that sort of thing because pretty ships sail, and then they go off course and end up docked for ghost tours. My mom probably still looks good, even though she has been cremated. I know her, and I'm sure she still looks good wherever she is (was that too dark? My mom would have cracked up).

In first grade, Mrs. Carter put up with me. She was friendly, and I liked her. She had dark hair and pretty clothes and shoes. She was tall and thin, and a pattern formed in my brain about who I could accept and who would be cast aside.

Second grade was Mrs. Thompson, and I adored her. She was a black woman, which was rare at Case Elementary School back in the sixties. I can't even imagine the shit she had to put up with to get there. I remember her as kind and attentive, and I used to hug her all the time. She was comforting, she didn't yell at me, and she was very patient.

Despite being raised in a home void of physical affection, I could be very affectionate with people I cared about. It was probably annoying. My parents never hugged anyone, but I hugged them both their entire lives. My sister never hugged anyone and still won't, but I made my parents endure my need for affection. By the time I was twenty-five, they were finally used to it and even hugged me back now and again instead of standing there confused. Oddly enough, I developed a very "don't hug me" vibe as an adult. I'm only fond of it if I know you. Being in the music business means many people come up to you and hug you, and it's sweet but can be very trying for me now. Whatever made me love with wild abandon has disappeared over time.

In third grade Mrs. Murphy told the principal I should be tested because she thought I may be on the spectrum (but there was a much more derogatory term used in the sixties). My grades were horrible. I couldn't learn, sit still, or concentrate, and I "didn't have friends." They didn't know about all my cousins at home, so that was bullshit. The whole busload from Appalachia had now procreated. I had friends aplenty; we just happened to be related.

Because of her, I was taken to a psychiatrist in third grade. I remember he had me do a drawing. I drew a horse, and he said it was remarkable, and I felt special. A letter from him saying I was of sound mind and more advanced than slow put her in her place.

I remember being very fond of the testing process, which was all about drawing pictures and talking about myself. I was also very fond of my doctor because he complimented and engaged me and paid attention. I ended up seeing him quite a bit as a child for my many emotional issues. I may have also had more going on than some schoolmates because I was forced to do so much alone. I was insanely independent because of how I was raised up to that point. I sometimes wonder if maybe I was indeed on the spectrum (would still be, I guess), and it just wasn't a thing then?

I had an intense fear of abandonment because my mom forgot to pick me up a few times after school. I once sat on the front stoop at Case Elementary in Akron, and I remember thinking, "Oh my God, they moved away! They left me! They are gone!" I really thought my family may have just left town without me. At times, I worried that my mom was in an accident and was in the hospital, and no one came to tell me. She felt so bad for forgetting to pick me up, and she apologized, but the damage was done, and my psychiatrist admonished her for it.

She used to tell people that the doctor really put her in her place and told her she caused my intense fear of abandonment. I remember being mad at my doctor for yelling at my mom, but he was pretty charming and he really liked my horse drawing, so my angst didn't last. Most of the time her tardiness or forgetfulness when it came to me getting home from school was because she was lost in her painting. My mother was a wonderful artist.

I had a stern, unfriendly teacher in fourth grade, Mrs. Warts (I made that name up on purpose). She wasn't a Tracey fan either, and it was around this time they decided to put me on a drug called Ritalin for hyperactivity. My mom gave it to me for about a week, then took me off of it. The drug caused me to sit and stare and not do much else. It zapped my will to live. My family missed me being me, and I never retook it. To this day, I am always on the fence about taking any medications, legal or otherwise. Don't get me wrong, I thoroughly enjoy a good downer (as we used to call them back in the day) because I am so high-strung that it's nice to mellow out now and again. But it doesn't mean I do that often. I am the only person I know who gets excited when I have to have surgery because I like "going under," as they say. I especially hate it when prescription mood drugs are dispensed to children before they have even had a chance to figure themselves out. It's criminal to drug children unless they really need it, and a lot of the time, they just might not.

Now, we come to fifth grade with Mrs. Hell (I made that name up on purpose as well, if the really bad shoe fits). Soon, the shit hit the fan. This woman caused me more trauma than any of them. She was terribly mean to me. She would always call me out in front of the class, and of course, they laughed at me. It was my worst year in school, and I remember it all too well.

I was not living the high life. I didn't know it; I was doing what I thought everyone else was doing. We moved constantly, sometimes sleeping in the car in rest areas or breaking into relatives' homes when they were on vacation. I had unstable parents, though my mom really did try, God bless her. I was an emotional wreck, only I didn't realize it. I wasn't getting any help with anything school-related, and I was suffering.

Looking back, it's evident—and a sad shame—that Mrs. Hell didn't bother looking a little deeper. She chastised me daily in front of everyone. She laughed at me constantly. She called on me to answer questions, and when I failed, they laughed.

Little Miss Akron

I went home for lunch once, and my pet bird had died (RIP PoPo). I was devastated! My mom didn't send me back to school; she let me stay home that afternoon and helped me put on my little bird's funeral. The next day, she wrote me a note: "Tracey had the afternoon off because her pet bird died, and I let her stay home because she was upset." Mrs. Hell read the letter out loud to the class and then mocked me, saying, "Oh, poor Tracey, her bird died." They all laughed at me.

I was so upset I peed myself. I peed myself in fifth grade, right there in my seat. Far past the age where one should let that rip. She made me go get newspapers, put them under my desk, and again, made fun of me. She did not let me go to the bathroom or get cleaned up. I had to sit in my pee on the newspaper, for everyone to see. I was absolutely the class freak, geek, clown, and outcast. Didn't they know I was *Little Miss Akron* AND *Fairlawn*? Only now, I was nothing but a ball of trauma trapped in the educational system that was my prison and personal hell, because of Mrs. Hell.

Sixth grade found me changing schools, which was rare. My unstable father made us move constantly, but my forever-trying-to-be-stable mother managed to find apartments in the same school district so as not to shuffle me about in the school system at least. My sister changed districts all the time, which was awful for her. She was a decade older than me, so her shuffle had ended by this point, but mine was ongoing. I ended up at Fort Island Elementary with Mr. Fredrick. I liked him so much. I had never had a male teacher; he was young, kind, patient, and pretty groovy.

My father had started a job that would last for a while, and he quit drinking for a few years. This mostly ended the moving about, and we bought a house right before my thirteenth birthday. Alas, the war's end was not on the horizon, but this battle was won.

In seventh grade, I flunked. I missed too many days. My mother was not doing well mentally, and she would keep me home so she wouldn't be alone. I was sent to seventh grade at Revere Junior High School for my second go-around, to keep me from being embarrassed by said flunkage at Copley Junior High School. It was a school close to our district, and we were literally living on the border. I had Copley kids on one side and Revere kids on the other.

I was in school with famed serial killer Jeffrey Dahmer but did not know him then. My friend Sisi did, and she was next to him in the yearbook, so I used to see her on the news when they showed his yearbook photos. They eventually discovered I was in the wrong district, so I returned to Copley. Middle school was a nightmare, and a girl named Fran said I was on her hit list. When I asked her why, she said I was weird. That sums up middle school.

I was very athletic during my years at Copley. I loved gymnastics, and it became my passion. I did the balance beam and floor routine. I had been taught dance from an early age because my mother, my Aunt Deane, and my sister were all professional dancers. They weren't strippers, mind you; they were ballroom dance teachers. It would have been okay if they were strippers, but they were not. My aunt and mom owned a studio in Akron and then Miami. They also worked together as a team for a bit at Fred Astaire Studios. Always as a team: you got Helen, and you got Deane.

I started doing well in high school, but only socially and never academically. I was cut from the diving team because of my grades. I was on the gymnastics team, but it was only an exhibition team, not competitive. I tried out for cheerleading but again was disqualified because of my grades.

Little Miss Akron

We had a house, now; roots, a place of our own. I made some friends, and they came over. We did typical teenage stuff: made out with a lot of boys, flicked class, went to parties, tried alcohol, and bought records at our local (Summit) Mall. The usual.

My best friend from age thirteen has always been Andrea Beckett. Remember this because she comes up a lot in this memoir. Our first experience drinking was at her house with her sister Patty and some Colt 45. We picked it because we had crushes on Billy Dee Williams, and he did the commercial, so it had to be good. God, was I sick the next day. I never was much of a drinker until my punk rock days, and to this day, wine is more my thing than beer (and it is indeed a thing).

We spent endless hours at Skyway Drive-In, which was the spot to hang out in my 'hood in the seventies, flirting with the curb boys and playing the radio loudly. After Andrea got her license, we were always there. I still can't believe that I'm alive to tell the story because of her terrible driving. When we reconnected after many years, one of my first questions was, "Are you still a horrible driver?" She said yes, and we noted that we were lucky to still be alive. We recently took a trip to visit her sister Patty in North Carolina, and, in her defense, she drove brilliantly.

Back then, we would drink beer while driving around listening to music (ARE YOU KIDDING ME?). That was the usual Saturday night. We made a pact: if a KC and The Sunshine Band song came on the radio, we had to pull over, get out, and dance no matter where we were. We did so many times in many strange places.

We grew apart for a bit after she got married and moved away. I sang at her wedding, and then off she went, and I started my life as a punk rocker. She recently put it this way: we are the only ones who know what it was like during that part of our lives. No one else who is close to us now was there for it. So this friendship is very special because we can discuss these memories. We totally get each other because we did it all together, all the firsts. Now in our sixties, probably all the lasts, too. Wow, I am macabre.

At some point around fifth grade, the FBI came to our house. We had a neighbor, Mr. Patrick, who was an FBI agent. His son Ron was my neighborhood friend, and I still know him. Mr. Patrick told my parents they were following a man who was a pedophile and had, assumedly, assaulted a few children. Apparently, he was stalking me, and they had tracked him via a private detective. Then, the FBI was on the case. My parents had to agree to a phone tap because they knew he had been calling. They had me walk home from school so they could follow him.

I was to walk with an older girl from the neighborhood, who was in on the whole thing. Looking back, she was probably not even a student, but one of the FBI agents. I remember him calling and talking to me on the phone, asking me questions, saying that he was with the police and that I was in trouble. I had thrown a rock at a car one day, and I was sure that he was calling to arrest me, so I believed him. I always told my parents, and they thought it was a kid pranking us. It turns out it was this poor excuse for a human. The detectives followed me home daily, waiting for this man to show up.

One day, he finally did.

A light yellow car with a white top pulled up and slowed down, keeping pace as I walked home after my walking mate went to her house a few doors down. He rolled down his window to talk to me, always saying he was with the police. The FBI had been watching, and they were suddenly by my side. Someone came to get me and walked me home the rest of the way.

Then, Mr. Patrick came to the house, and the adults said he had been caught. He was in prison, and what we did to help was a big deal. I could have been a victim, but they saved my life.

I guess Mrs. Hell wasn't my biggest problem in the fifth grade, after all.

Quite fashionable, even in the fourth grade. January 15, 1969

FOUR SEASONS

Written by Tracey Thomas
From the 2000 album *Lights*

Here comes the night,
I guess it's time to turn on the lights.

You are as cold as anyone that I have ever known,
You're like a December wind across a New York street.
I'm always overheating, just like the August sun,
I'm always beating down, beating down on everyone.

Prechorus
But you're drawn to me, and I'm drawn to you,
Stranger things have happened.

Chorus
Four seasons give me, four seasons give me,
Four seasons give me change.
Four seasons give me, four seasons give me,
Four seasons give me four reasons to stay.

You are the tiny light of hope, that keeps me hanging 'round,
You're like an angel in my dream, that never makes a sound.
But I'm not the answer you seek, that brick don't have to fall,
And I won't have to bang my head against the wall.

Well, I don't think you understand,
Just how strong I really am,
And I don't think you give a damn anyway.

About Four Seasons: *This song is about the opposites in people and relationships. You are this, I am that, and somehow it still works. It's about compromising, trying, failing, and not giving up.*

My husband and I are very different, like...very. He is calm, unattached to outcomes, mellow, and hard to fluster. I am nervous, attached to what I perceive as outcomes, high-strung, and very easy to fluster. We should never have worked; we really shouldn't have. Thirty years later, and we are still friends and partners. I honestly wasn't sure when I wrote this song in the nineties if that would be the case because we were not exactly right for each other on paper. Our love for family, music, movies with happy endings, and our strong friendship made it all work.

I have always been really proud of this one. I like the structure, and the musicians killed it. A nod to guiarist John Gildersleeve and John Sferra, the incomparable drummer from Glass Harp, for making "Four Seasons" what it is.

THREE:
BABY, SOMETIMES LOVE JUST AIN'T ENOUGH

My first marriage was as brutal as my upbringing. I married Tony, the handsome, reckless lead singer of Trudee and the Trendsetters, a popular area band during the "Akron Sound" days. I was young and in love, and it seemed normal to me.

We hit it off from day one. We were the local "it" couple. We'd sing "I Got You Babe" together. We even made the paper when we got married. We thought we were rock stars, and we looked the part. Punk Rock Barbie and her Billy Idol lookalike, conquering the world...of Akron.

We lived in Firestone Park, an area of Akron that had seen better days but was gritty and acceptable enough for two rebellious punks. One cashier at our little Sparkle Market grocery store always called us her "Hollywood couple" and told us how beautiful we were and that we should be in movies. She didn't seem to mind the leather, safety pins, and ripped clothes. Most of the other customers in the store stared and looked scared, and the older people sneered at us. I get it: we tried too hard. We looked like we wanted to start a fight, but really, we just needed to buy bread. Trying to be noticed for my fierceness and confidence was all a big scam. I had neither, but I was very good at playing the role.

Tony was terribly hard on me, and the sad part is that it didn't seem unusual. He criticized my band, Unit 5, and would get mad when we got shows he felt his band was better suited for. When we opened for The Dead Boys a few times, Tony would make fun of me, saying we were a terrible fit. Their lead singer/songwriter, Stiv Bators, requested that we open the shows. He liked us, and we were thrilled about it,

Little Miss Akron

but I always felt guilty.

Tony was not overly warm and fuzzy. He was sarcastic and had no filter. He said what he thought, and sometimes it was harsh. He suffered from terrible depression and extreme shyness. He drank to ease his struggles with people and with himself. He would sometimes drink a whole case of beer in a day, more often a twelve-pack. After five beers, he was open, kind, friendly, and fun. By the time he drank nine beers, his mood turned darker, and I got the brunt of it. Never physically, he was not "that guy." I tried very hard, and we made it seven years before I had to leave. By this point, we had a son, Cory, and I could not justify raising him in such a hostile environment. I wanted his life to be the polar opposite of mine, so I had to go. It wasn't easy—it was horrible, actually—but I had to do what was best for our mental health. It ended very badly. More on that later.

My mother was severely agoraphobic for well over a decade during my formative years. While she had a good heart and a wicked amount of charisma, during her menopausal years, she was crippled by panic attacks, phobias, and—what was termed then—nervous breakdowns. Most of the time, she tended to prioritize her needs over everyone else's, including mine. It was a lot to deal with.

My father, to my child's mind, was dark and scary. The things he was talented in (gifted, even) were not what most men of that era were passionate about, yet no one knew that about him. He worked, married, and did what was expected of him. He even joined the army as a paratrooper.

He also played nearly every instrument, made my mother's dresses, was an excellent chef, and painted like a master. He was complex, talented, brilliant, and just a nightmare of a human to live with. Years later, after he died, we got a letter from what turned out to be his male partner, who we knew as his best friend, and it all clicked into place.

The world did not kill my love for it despite being raised by him, and I am happy about that. I desperately want to be understood by people who know me and are confused by me. Hell, I'm confused by me, too. It seems like explaining how I was formatted will go a long way in painting that picture.

I have never doubted that my family (both the one I was born into and the one I have created) loves me. I have known a lot of love, even though some came with a flawed delivery. Tony loved me. My mom loved me. But I didn't know my dad did until later in life. I thought there was just a big void there, but it turns out he was capable of something other than cruelty, but only just a little bit.

I now know all of these people had mental health issues that caused them to make some bad decisions, and there was fallout from that. I believe that an inability to love correctly is tied to mental health and wellness. Yet living with mental health issues does not necessarily mean you'll end up alone, institutionalized, sad, afraid, or—the absolute worst of all—ignored.

Love is a conundrum. It can be fully awake and present yet still be misguided or hurtful. Sometimes, as the song goes, love just ain't enough. It is limitless when it is good and healthy; when it is flawed and obsessive, it is the opposite. Through all this brutal love, I know that if I can rise from my ashes, anyone can.

My parents, Jim and Helen Thomas

Usually Love

Written by Tracey Thomas
From the 2020 album *My Roots Are Showing*

Well, I knew there'd be trouble, and I knew it long ago.
When I let you have your way, with my heart and with my soul.
Well my Mama cried, said you were no good,
and of course she was right, you were bothered.
But I knew somehow, it would all work out,
though I was damned one way or the other.

Chorus
So I said, row your boat ashore and lay with me,
In the dark of night, beneath the tallest tree.
Take your heavy heart and give me some room,
To light the way and ignite the gloom.
Every now and then, we all lose our mind,
And it's usually love that's behind it.

Well, we danced a while and then we walked for miles,
With no worry of the world behind us.
Then the sun come up just like it always does.
And it brings the wising up along with it.
Oh, I loved you once and I loved you much,
but there's no fixing what is damned to stay broken.

About Usually Love: *This song is about my first husband, Tony, and how I really should have thought it through better before we married. I knew it would be rough. We were young punk rockers in bands, living that life.*

My mom did NOT want me to marry him. He was sarcastic, drank too much, did drugs, and didn't treat me very well. He had his demons, and I had mine too. His were really dark at times; mine were dark but tried to be pretty. I saw them in the mirror with pink lipstick and bows in their hair. I gave them the option to be better; I thought they had possibilities. Tony's demons knew the end game and didn't appreciate my optimism.

We had some wonderful times together. We talked about everything, went for long walks, socialized with friends, and tried to make life normal and functional. We really did have love; he loved me despite the flawed delivery, but in the end, as with many things in life, my mom was right.

FOUR:
CANCER SUN, SCORPIO RISING, LIBRA MOON

July 12, 1959, 4:38 PM. I was born with a veil.

The doctor told my mother that certain belief systems think that being born with a caul over your face (the technical name would be "membrane," but that's not overly glamorous) signifies psychic abilities. He also told her that I was a little psychic, before he told her I was a girl. Some Native American tribes felt, and probably still do, that babies born with a caul should be raised to be spiritual leaders or shamans. Many tribal cultures worldwide have the same belief: that the child should be raised as a prophet, healer, or spiritual leader.

I have been plagued by visions and "knowings" my whole life. I have found it embarrassing for most of said life, so I've never opened up about it much. I see all these fraudulent idiots on television, on the internet, and in newspapers, books, and magazines. I did not ever want to be associated with that. A tight little group of people knew that I had these odd tendencies, and they respected my need and my right to be vague about it. For one, it scared me and made me feel insane at times. My dreams, visions, thoughts, and knowings were confusing to me. I felt like I had to keep it to myself, and I did. Still, I wish I had opened the conversation far earlier in life because it has been fascinating and integral to who I am today.

Having a mother who was institutionalized time and again made me fearful that anything that was not a normal, day-to-day kind of life would raise a red flag over my head, and then I would be the next subject of an unwanted conversation.

That was an uphill battle in and of itself. I did not want anyone to turn this "gift" I seemed to have into something it wasn't, so I held that close to the vest for most of my life.

I was always interested in "witchy" things like ghosts, tarot, seances, and the paranormal in general. It wasn't just me, either. My sister Sandy and I are both wired that way, and we've messed with some things we shouldn't have, including some organized religions with a "culty" side.

My grandmother was a southern Appalachian Baptist who thought demons were around every corner. I was in ninth grade when a teacher at Copley Junior High School decided to do a little experiment in class. She had students, one at a time, leave the room to stand in the hall while the other students concentrated on a card that was held up for the class. Regular playing cards. The person in the hall would come back in and tell the class what card they thought she was holding after trying to hone in on it out in the hall. Apparently, I killed it. My teacher (I've long since forgotten her name, but she looked like Kim Novak) called my mother and told her I had intuitive ability and thought I should be tested professionally.

Well, that went over like a ton of bricks. My mother, at the time, was an in-denial paranormal enthusiast, having been raised by said southern Baptists from Appalachia, and she thought my teacher had crossed a line. I thought it was the most fun I had ever had in school—except for grilled cheese and tomato soup day. My mom made a stink and called the school. The teacher was disciplined, and that class (Language Arts, I believe) was restructured. From that point forward, it did not include experimenting with psychic abilities.

Years later, I reconnected with this teacher and discovered she was highly interested in the paranormal. Apparently, my mom almost got her fired, and many parents were not thrilled with her. I believe her class was the beginning of my love for all things related to the occult. Only, not demons. I don't entertain that. The scariest movie I have ever seen to this day is *The Omen*. No demonology, please, and thank you. If you want to talk about anything else, I am open. I told my dentist that I thought I had an alien implant in my nose, and she said it was doubtful. Like I said, I will talk about any of it. Just not Damien or Gregory Peck.

After turning fifty, I slowly embraced this oddity in my life. I turned it into a very normal, positive way of being. I started studying all kinds of paranormal and metaphysical subjects in earnest. I educated myself even further (it had already been a lifelong reading subject of mine), and I now have a wealth of knowledge about "things that go bump in the night."

I have come to call myself the catastrophe prophet. For some reason, I hone in on global disasters. They are not on speed dial; I didn't see the September 11 tragedy coming. However, I did foresee the 1986 Challenger space shuttle explosion, an earthquake in China in 1976, the Covid-19 pandemic (My dad warned me about it in a dream), and, more recently, the 2023 earthquake in Turkey and Syria.

I am wired to randomly pick up on global tragedies, usually about 48 hours prior. Many times, that 48-hour window passes, and nothing happens. But it is still tough to wrap my head around when it does happen. It is certainly not something that is written in stone. I get a lot of premonitions that fizzle out, which is a good thing, given my propensity for disasters. As mentioned, I've experimented and explored this side of myself since around the age of eleven when my teacher opened that can of worms. Then, by the age of thirteen, my sister and I flirted with the dark side together in between bouts of being church-going Christians because we scared ourselves half to death. I was pretty hooked.

Little Miss Akron

Today, I read tarot for clients all over the damn place (thank you, internet), from as far away as Israel and England. I love what I do. It is a lovely way to spend my "older chick" days.

I have never seen what I would call a stereotypical ghost or UFO, which really bums me out. I'm still waiting. I have had what I refer to as a "time slip." I also had an experience with a shapeshifter, which was mind-blowing. I have had an experience which could be considered a "spirit," with a Native American man in a pumpkin field in Copley, Ohio. I will never really know; he was a solid human being and not at all what you would think of as a spirit. Many of my experiences involve a Native American "vibe," including a genuine vision of myself in a previous life as an elderly Native American man in the Red Rocks.

You may want to stop reading now, having read that bit. It reminds me of when I read Shirley MacLaine's *Don't Fall Off The Mountain* (I think, but one of her books anyway). There was a story where she said someone took over driving the car for her when she was in danger, and I was like, "YEAH RIGHT!" Then the shit hit the fan for me a few years later when I stepped over the line of what I knew to be reality (Not too far over–like, Jesus never took my wheel—but a little over the line). Shirley will always be one of my absolute favorite actresses, and I adore her books, movies, and personality. Who knows, maybe Jesus does drive; he sure seems to do a lot of remarkable things.

I also had a vision of a young, very handsome, Turkish man, who was a whirling dervish. I knew it was me. It clicked in my head that I was him, somewhere along the space-time continuum. I could feel and remember it just like a memory from this Tracey experience, but it was not. It's odd and may not be connected, but throughout my life, I have dreamt of spinning in a dance that made me feel euphoric. I was dancing and spinning, and it was magic. Sadly, these dreams stopped happening about ten years ago.

I have also had horrific issues with positional vertigo for most of my life. I have been tested, medicated, and laid up with this disorder. It does make me wonder if there is a connection to a previous incarnation. I believe truth is relative; rather, like a diet, not one is right for everyone. We all work within our own experience to get what we need. My theory about reincarnation is a bit out there because I think we may be able to tap into a life we choose and that maybe many people have experienced the same life by choice. This is a theory I have had for a couple of decades. It's all a simulation, and we essentially control it or play it from somewhere else. I have many ideas about what life is and is not. My only real conclusion is that this one life experience is probably not all there is to it.

My mother was a little wild, but at her core, she was still a child of the mountains: religious and scared to death that she would sin and go to hell. It did not keep her from the Italian men she loved or from drinking the nights away at swanky clubs with her sister and cousins. She did not, however, mess with the sin of the paranormal. Until she did.

One day, she came to my sister and me and said she also had this little gift from our female ancestors. We were like, "What the hell!?" It did not fit our perception of our mother, and it shocked us. We spent the day talking about her most profound vision; that of a young, tall, black, barefoot man in overalls, one strap hanging down. She knew, in her soul, that it was her, just like me with my past-life visions. She never told anyone until that day.

My mother also said she had a weird thing happen where she experienced her arms and legs lifting off the bed. She didn't understand it and, again, didn't tell anyone for a long time. I believe she felt possessed for a while; I know it scared her. Then she told us how Aunt Ivory and some of the cousins from Virginia used to levitate objects and have seances. My grandmother was not privy to that information and would have struck them down in the name of Jesus (I am not making fun of Jesus; I just think he would have been okay with some of this stuff). My grandmother, however, was best left in the dark about certain things.

Aunt Ivory was my Gram Hattie's sister and she was way ahead of her time. She was outspoken, hilarious, bawdy and unfiltered. She didn't have that religious dogma the rest of the family suffered from, yet they endured. In some extremely religious families, you're just made to feel guilty about being alive. Again, I'm not throwing shade at Christians. I love the Jesus stories, my own self. However, I do not think organized religions are a positive force on this planet. When you throw conservative politics into your church requirements, I'll take a hard pass. It's not a match made in your stereotypical heaven.

Back to my Aunt Ivory. She read tea leaves, hosted seances, and read tarot cards and palms, sometimes on the down low and sometimes very openly. She also identified as a Christian, she just didn't turn it into an immovable fence around her life. Aunt Ivory spoke of levitating a refrigerator with some cousins at one of the paranormal nights she hosted. They didn't call it that back then; they were just seances, during exploration with the spiritualist movement. The cousins and her siblings gave her so much grief about messing with it. Still, she did what she wanted to do. Apparently, she wanted to lift heavy appliances.

It's actually odd that we never did anything else with this information. Just talking about it here now, I realize I haven't mentioned it much before. We just cataloged those stories and returned to business as usual, like "cool stuff, levitating a refrigerator, no big deal." They swear it happened. I remain a little skeptical because I didn't see it, but this wasn't a group of people who were overly fond of lying. Lie=sin=hell. My family tree has some magic in the roots. My experiences were real, so maybe the fridge actually did fly, who knows?

We were finally told about my mom's abilities because she was flat broke and trying to keep our house on Smith Road after my dad took off (again) to Florida. He left her with nothing, and she was panic-stricken about possibly losing our house. She fessed up because she wanted my sister to get her a job with The Psychic Friends Network. A big deal then; they were a company that did over-the-phone psychic readings if you called a 1-900 number. My sister had great success working for them, and she got me a job, too, and I loved it.

My sister was the psychic reader on the television infomercial with Dionne Warwick back in the day. She rode that wave to Los Angeles for a week to film the infomercial and hobnob. Because of that appearance, she developed a great following at home in Akron and over the phone. She also read for a member—he who shall not be named—of The Grateful Dead, which I thought was pretty groovy. She read for Dionne herself and some politicians here and there, too.

Eventually, after seeing we were making a living, my mom said she could do it too and that it was probably "okay with God." They seemed to have a conversation about it, and he or she gave her the go-ahead. So she interviewed and, like Sandy and I, got the gig. The interview involved doing a reading for one of the higher-ups. You had to be spot-on to get work with them. It may seem really scammy, and it was in a few aspects (especially the cost and how we were told to keep people on the line to rack up the money). But some great readers were working there. I don't mean to frighten you, but there are more of us than you think. I should wink here; only you can't tell if I am or not. I am, by the way, winking right now.

They did test you a few times before you were hired. I only did this because I needed a job so badly. I was divorced at that time and raising a son on my own. I was not able to work and pay for daycare and have anything left at all. After taking two years to complete a nine-month cosmetology course (always overachieving), I worked as a hairdresser for a while, only to spend all the money on daycare. That didn't make sense then, and it still doesn't.

Working from home was not a common thing back then, but this gave me that very opportunity. My mom watched Cory a lot, but for me to go to work and leave him all day with her when she was still unable to drive was iffy. She would also fall asleep on occasion because the meds made her so tired. I had to find work and have daycare, so it was a win-win situation; I stayed home with him and still made a living. I knew I would never con or lie to anyone, so I worked the lines my own way, knowing the higher-ups listened in now and again. They wanted us to keep people on the line so they would have to pay more, and I was failing miserably.

I met some great people, did some great readings, had some great reviews, and eventually left. Ultimately, I didn't cut it in the "sales" department and my numbers weren't great when it came to total minutes per call. I still do some readings and I try my best to make life better for people questioning the Universe. I am not really a go-getter. I am more of a "you bring it here" kind of person, but if I had been, I could have made a living as a reader. I need enough to get by, and I'm not greedy or ambitious. But I know tarot, and I am wired to connect with people.

My favorite, most intense story from my paranormal life happened shortly after my first husband, Tony, died. Until now, I think only three people knew this story. I have kept it close because it is all at once unbelievable and reality-busting.

By reading thus far, you know that I hate to be misunderstood. You also know I have struggled with some mental health issues, so you may chalk it up to that. I can, however, tell you that at the age of sixty-five, with much counseling, reflecting, talking, and living behind me, I have a couple of issues that do not involve hallucinating, hearing voices, or seeing things.

I am a member of the extreme PTSD club, with a special backstage pass for raging obsessive compulsive disorder. Neither of which would explain what happened to me on a Native American reservation in 1992.

Cory and I took a road trip. We used to do that together when he was just a little guy, before he started school, but old enough to get something out of it. We headed south to Gatlinburg, Tennessee, to meet my beloved cousin Kat, who was living in Florida. Her family moved away when I was about eleven or twelve, and it broke my heart. We were best friends; our families even shared a duplex at one point. We kept the apartment doors open and ran amuck between the units. We were like sisters. Her daughter Tracy is named after me, and my daughter is named Emma Katherine as a nod to her.

I hadn't seen her in what felt like forever, so we agreed to meet in Gatlinburg for a holiday. She brought her wonderful husband, Paul. We had a lovely visit, and before heading home, I decided to take a detour to the Qualla Boundary in the Cherokee lands of North Carolina, Blue Ridge Mountains. I liked the energy of Native American land, so I've visited a few different places in the north and south to experience that. I have always been so deeply connected to Native American culture.

We grew up knowing that my grandmother, Delilah Hensley, was born on a reservation in Oklahoma City. She was darker-skinned with long, black, silky, poker-straight hair that ran to her waist. She looked the part, and we accepted that as part of our heritage. She was supposedly Melungeon, meaning part Cherokee, part European, and part African. There is only one photo of her and I don't have it. She was afraid the camera would steal her soul and refused to be photographed. My DNA test revealed an unusual amount of all the "white" things. I was a little bummed because I was raised believing that my heritage was Melungeon, too.

Little Miss Akron

I traveled from Gatlinburg to North Carolina with a six-year-old with me in my cute white convertible. The trip was not overly memorable to begin with. I just wanted to bask in the energy of the land. I was very into meditating back then, and Cory was very into sleeping, so it worked out.

I went to breakfast at the local diner the day I was set to leave. Before I left, the man at the table next to me started a conversation, so I decided I could hang out for a few more minutes. He, of course, mentioned Cory's hair, which was a white bush of curly fantasticness. That hair got us a lot of attention. Sarah McLachlan and I took a little walk together once, and she kept playing with his hair. My second (and current) husband Scott knew Sarah, so we were backstage before she played a show in Cleveland. She also kissed my daughter Emma on the head when she was six weeks old. I teased that she would be a singer, since Sarah branded her, and–funny enough–Emma is one hell of a singer. But I digress.

There were two men at a table next to us: one was a younger man, older than me at the time, and one was very old. He introduced the older man as Crow and said it was either his father or grandfather; I can't remember for sure. He noted that Crow wanted to tell me he would see me soon. I said something like, "Oh, that's so sweet, but we leave today. Just have to pay the bill and then off we go back to Ohio."

The younger man said something to him then, to me: "He insists that he will see you again." I smiled at the old guy and just said, "Okay."

He looked at me in a way that made me shiver. He turned to face me head-on, and I realized he was missing an eye. He was so wrinkly and tan. It wasn't exactly creepy, but he wasn't NOT creepy either. I remember the younger man admonishing him, claiming he was a big tease and that this was his norm: to mess with the tourists.

I said my goodbyes and went to the car, loaded my son, and headed off. On the road out, I was solo—no other cars—on a pretty remote dirt road. Suddenly, a giant black bird landed in front of my car. It was so big I remember pondering if it was a raven or a black bird, if there was actually a difference, and if one was bigger. It just sat there. I couldn't go around it without possibly hitting it, so I waited. I yelled out the window and then honked the horn. I remember it was wickedly early, and I was trying to get close to home before dark. I finally got out of the car and confronted the beast, trying to shoo it away. I was standing inside my door because I was afraid to approach it. Cory was still in the car.

I ended up turning off the car and locking the doors so no one could jump out of the trees and kidnap my son (welcome to my head). I walked closer to this annoying bird, who by now was pissing me off. I am sure I said something like, "Hey, nice bird, I must go now. You need to move." That is what I do: I talk to the animals as if they know what I mean. I did it yesterday to a large raccoon I thought was a dog until closer inspection. I don't like raccoons, so that was really a moment.

Then the dumb bird turned toward me and (drum roll please) had one eye. He made a rather loud noise, then off he went. You know how sometimes when you are panic-stricken or shocked, you just freeze? That happened, but it wasn't fear so much as shock. What the fuck?!

I stood there, trying to comprehend what I was experiencing. I don't even remember watching it fly off. I remember seeing the missing eye and knowing I had just encountered a shapeshifter.

That old man, who was introduced to me as CROW from the diner, who said he would see me again with that little laugh of his, whose son/grandson had told him to stop it, had just seen me again. That bird made a point of showing me his missing eye. I wasn't scared; I was shocked, frozen. I did not know what to do with my new information about the meaning of life, and I still don't. Then, I got in my car and drove home. It may all be a coincidence. Or maybe Jesus took my wheel right there so I could have the sign I had always begged for from the Universe and Shirley MacLain. To this day, I don't know what that was, but it absolutely felt like Crow, the old man from the diner. Now ya know.

My second most profound paranormal experience is one I call "Field of Dreams." I absolutely love Halloween (of course I do). I always took Cory to large, farm-vibe pumpkin patches to pick out his pumpkin. Later, Scott and I would take our kids to different pumpkin patches, which was a big deal in our family.

When Cory was about six years old, we went to get our pumpkins. I remember running into one of my best friends from my teens and twenties, Diane, in the parking lot. We chatted for a minute; she was on her way out, and I was on my way in. I went to the counter to check-in. Behind me was a man a little older than myself, mid to late thirties. He stood there, and I felt like he was working at the farm and was going to show me out to the patch, but I remember thinking that was dumb. It was right there, and this wasn't my first rodeo. I didn't say anything. I just started heading out to the field.

Cory looked at all the pumpkins along the way, trying to decide what he wanted. We kept going out, further and further. We just kept walking. The guy was with us the whole time, but not really with us, just walking along. It wasn't remote, and I didn't get bad vibes from him. I guess I thought he was going to help us carry should we get a large one. I kept looking back and thought it was odd he wasn't engaging or talking to me. I'm sure I smiled or greeted him.

In my mind, it felt like we were miles away from the parking lot, the three of us in a rowboat on an ocean of pumpkins. Eventually, Cory picked his white (really) pumpkin. I had two smaller ones for my dining table. I looked around for the man, and he was completely gone. I looked right, left, back, front. I even looked up. It was insane. Where did he go?

Even if he had walked back (or started to) since I last saw him there, he would be visible in one direction, no matter where he went. There were a few other people out in the field, here and there, pumpkin shopping. None of them were that guy. It was against the law of physics. This man could not have been there when I turned around and then gone when I looked again. He could have been a few yards in any direction but could not have returned to the store or out of that field.

I did the same thing as when I encountered Crow: I stood there frozen, trying to understand it. I didn't. I don't even remember asking Cory if he saw the man. There was no reason to do so because I am sure he did. The guy was with us the entire time.

My whole life, I have wanted to see a ghost. I know, it's weird. When I think about this, I never feel like it was a ghost experience because this was just a man—a very attractive man. I actually found him quite fetching, with a very Native American vibe. He was solid, human, real flesh and blood, and then he was none of that. More than likely, he was a ghost.

In my research over the years, I have read about many manifestations where the ghost appeared solid, real, and not made of vapors like your stereotypical specter. There is no explaining it, really. Now, I am waiting for a "spirit" kind of ghost, all translucent and ethereal. Scott has seen a few of those. The most honest, no-bullshit man has a couple of stories that give you the heebie-jeebies. Those are not mine to tell, but I believe every word that comes from his mouth. Unless you ask how many beers he has had, which is always and forever, just two. Aside from that, he's a truth-teller to a fault.

Little Miss Akron

Right before the 2020 pandemic, Scott and I were sitting at the drive-thru of a McDonald's (Market Street in Akron by the Lebron James "I Promise" school. You know the one, Akron peeps). We were waiting for what was probably coffee (Scott hates fast food). I looked up and saw a group of people on the corner across the street doing some sort of group photo.

They wore black robes with white ruffle collars. They also seemed to be wearing those odd little white wigs they wear in British court systems. One had an old camera on a tripod with the fabric/canvas piece pulled over his head. It didn't seem normal, so I thought they might be filming a movie or doing a commercial. I said, "What are they doing?" I looked at Scott and laughed a little. He asked who I was talking about, and I pointed across the street. Nothing and nobody was there. Nada. None. Bam. Boom. Just gone, like the man in the pumpkin patch.

Guess what I did? I froze. I was so shocked. Where did they go? I explained to Scott that they were not really of this time and place. They had very old-school legal profession garb on, and the camera was on a tripod with a man behind it. That guy also had a black robe; I remember that specifically. He may have side gigs in the ethereal as a photographer and lawyer. I researched it and found no legal organization in Akron that wore those robes and wigs. I will never know what that was, but the closest thing I found to explain it is referred to as a time slip. Scott knows me to be honest about my paranormal dealings because I will not create bad karma for myself by lying. Life is hard enough; I don't need the next one to be too. We just drove away saying, "That was weird." Another Tracey experience in the books.

I have more stories of this sort, but that isn't necessarily what the book is about, and I tend to get rather long-winded. It's ironic because I'm asthmatic.

Ghost Town

Written by Tracey Thomas
From the 2007 album *Ghost Town*

Dark and dusty, damp and musty,
This whole world has got me down.
Cold and lonely, feeling only,
The wind pulling me to the ground.

Chorus
Life ain't sweet in this old ghost town,
I'm just a shadow of myself.
Horns of plenty blowing in my ear,
But I don't hear a sound.

Dawn is breaking, I am chasing,
The elusive light behind your eyes.
Run for cover, just another,
Frightened deer in the headlights.

Dancing restless like a girl,
Like the girl I used to be.
Handsome stranger leaves me breathless,
But I'm invisible — no one can see me.

About Ghost Town: *I recorded this album when I was knee-deep in the middle of caring for my mother, who was battling cancer. I had three young children, five pets, and a big house on an acre of land that I tended to by myself. I felt out of it, brought on by the stress of life, so I took to my notebook and guitar.*

This entire record has that feeling to me, filled with an energy of being worn down, worn out, but still going. In a way, I hope it does. For me, the feeling is as important as, or even more important than, the technical ability to deliver it.

FIVE:
SONGS FROM THE WOMB

My maternal grandmother was from Appalachia, and her parents and their parents were too. Everyone eventually settled in Richlands, Tazewell County, Virginia, for hundreds of years. We descended from the White family who came here on the Mayflower. My sister, my cousin Linda, and I were the first generation of our family born outside of Virginia. We are descendants of Colonel Robert "Potato Hole" Woodson, our grandfather (eight generations back I believe). His was a very interesting story in American history. He was known as "Potato Hole" Woodson because his mother hid him in a potato bin during the raid that killed his father. Having said that, my grandmother would beat our asses for believing in any juju. It was a sin, period.

When I was an infant and all through my growing years, my grandmother always had me over for sleepovers; we would make biscuits and drink Welch's grape juice, and I loved it until it got dark outside. As night would fall, I always freaked out, so I had to be picked up every single time. The point is that we were very close, my Gram and I. She always told the family stories about rocking me and singing to me. She insisted that I would babble the same back to her, repeating the melody to the best of my infantile ability, mimicking what she sang. I guess it was shocking to her. She, of course, felt it was a little unsettling because, in her world, anything that could not be explained was the devil. All these years later, I'm still singing; before I could talk, after I could talk, before I could walk, after I could walk.

My grandmother ended up being a wickedly wonderful influence in my life. We loved each other greatly—once she realized a singing baby wasn't necessarily possessed. She lived long enough to see me have some success in my music career, and she repeatedly told that story about how I was born into it and how it used to be spooky to her.

Later in life, after I became interested in genealogy, I discovered that my father's family was filled with musicians. I am proud of my Virginian roots on my mother's side and my Virginian and Tennessean roots on my father's side. My family has ancestors all over Virginia, Tennessee, and some in Kentucky for seasoning. I am, overall, a significantly displaced Southern gal. I do not, however, love the stories of the enslaved people some of them owned or their involvement in the Klu Klux Klan. Those stories are despicable and sickening to me. Human beings were handed down to sons like property.

It is really shocking to explore where you come from and the people you come from. Our only option is to live differently, to be aware of how you impact every person in your life, community, and personal space. If you are not compassionate and aware, you are cultivating an atmosphere of neglect. Unaware, without compassion, self-absorbed. That seems like history repeating itself, and I am unwilling to do that. Sins of the father, and all of that. Unfortunately, my forefathers had plenty of sins that the women have been trying to undo for generations.

One shock in my journey was very positive and came out of nowhere. My father's mother, Delila, is a controversial character in our family, and lordy mercy did she have secrets! One fun and interesting thing about the Hensley family that I learned later in life took me by surprise. I received a letter from a paternal relative telling me we were from the same family as the late country music legend Patsy Cline, who was also a Hensley. Grandma Delila was from that same family. That news blew me away, and I have since found a few connections to her. The connection is slight: a sixth cousin, maybe, but it's there.

Jesse James is a little closer in relation on my father's side, which explains a lot. I am also, related on my mom's side to the Hatfields (of Hatfields and McCoys fame), Blake Shelton (lots of Sheltons on that side of the family), and Richard Nixon (yay). My mother was born Helen Louise Nixon. My poor Uncle Dick was named Richard Nixon, and when all of the Watergate mess went down, he got a lot of attention he didn't want. His son Rick (also Richard Nixon) made the Akron Beacon Journal just for visiting the hospital when he was young. "Richard Nixon in hospital in Akron," or something like that. We couldn't escape it.

My mother always said I should take the country music train, even though she felt it was the music of the lower deck of the Titanic, and she had upper-deck dreams. She said that country vibe was in my voice. I finally embraced it in my sixties. I was long past my marketable phase by about thirty years, but I did it. In 2020, I released a rootsy Americana album called *My Roots Are Showing*, which was decades in the making. If I do it again (and God willing, I can), I may "twang" it up even more. You can take the girl out of Virginia, but you can't take Virginia out of the girl.

One of my first influences was Tanya Tucker. I loved her madly, and I still do. I lean that way a lot: Patty Loveless, Trisha Yearwood, Patsy Cline. I am not a big fan of the current pop/country hybrid, but there are still some artists I genuinely love in that world.

It's taken me so long to finish this book that things keep evolving well past the initial writing. Self-reflection is an interesting thing. This book journey began three years ago, and I keep returning to it, adding, subtracting, and re-evaluating things. I love that one of those things that I can add is a new acoustic record under my belt that I made with my longtime collaborator, producer, and friend, Ryan Humbert. It brings me joy and it scratches something off my bucket list. More on that later.

I still must make it to London, see the northern lights, and have a cup of coffee with Bono, which may keep my list active long term, because, that's doubtful. Or maybe wine with Bono? Cooked carrots are my least favorite food on this planet, but I would eat them with Bono. I think that would be a weird requirement on his part, eating cooked carrots with Tracey Thomas.

Bono, patiently waiting to have wine with me.

YESTERDAY'S CHILD

Written by Tracey Thomas
From the 1996 album *The Poet Tree*

Beyond all reason I can find,
The demons pray inside my mind,
Don't ask me questions, I've lost my direction,
And you can't wait for me to find it.

The pastels splashed upon the wall,
Don't have that calm effect at all,
I see their beauty, but it's somehow muted,
And I feel wild but not so free.

Chorus
Who will I be today?
Yesterday's child has gone away.
Where will I go tomorrow?
Yesterday's child loves her sorrow,
Yesterday's child.

The rite of passage just went wrong,
I guess I've known it all along,
Can't hide the fire, behind the liar,
And I can't wait for you to find it.

About Yesterday's Child: *"Yesterday's Child" was, at first, a poem about living with a clouded view of reality, being in a dark place, and being unable to see the light. It was actually about being institutionalized with depression. My mother went through that, and this song is mainly about her.*

The line "The pastels splashed up on the wall, don't have that calm effect at all" refers to her telling me the rooms were painted in certain pastel colors to set a calming mood for the patients.

"I see their beauty, but it's somehow muted" is a reference to her saying she just couldn't find joy in anything, including her art. She was a wonderful artist but, at times, just couldn't hear the muse.

SIX:
INSTABILITY IS THE NEW STABILITY

My father was a raging alcoholic, genius, musician, inventor, artist, car salesman, and generally a son of a bitch eighty percent of the time. I will give him twenty percent because he could be nice in the mornings after he got drunk. But he was a very angry man. I will keep going back to parental dynamics. It plays into so many things, so hang with me, people.

My mother and I estimated that we lived in at least thirty different places before I reached the age of twelve. We were constantly renting apartments and staying until evicted. My dad would fake his way through an application, and we were on to the next one for a couple of months—rinse and repeat. There was no internet then, and he was a very savvy con man.

Once, we stayed at (broke into) my Aunt Ivory's home on Delia Avenue in Akron for months while she wintered in Florida, and she never knew. There was no electricity; all the utilities were shut off while she was away. The feeling of being cold or seeing cold children freaks me out to this day. I'm always covering everybody up. I wake up at night to make sure my family hasn't kicked off the covers. I am always worried about someone being hungry or cold because I have been both.

Back then, through all of it, I had my dog Jacques. Somehow, my mom managed to keep him with us from place to place, lying on applications that demanded "no pets." She must have known he was the only stable thing I had going for me. My entire life has found me embracing dogs as my best friends, and they have always given me a sense of security that nothing else ever has. In a way, I was, quite literally, raised by wolves.

Little Miss Akron

In an odd twist of fate, I recently had some issues with my lungs. I had to have some allergy testing, and for the first time in my life, I am now terribly allergic to dogs. I still have my fifteen-year-old mutt Gibbard at home, but knowing he is my swan song is odd. I can't even imagine not having a dog in the house, yet that is the road I find myself on. God, I'm going to need another therapist.

My father was verbally abusive, and, at times, he seemed like he was going to wallop me, as my Gram used to say. He never hit anyone; he would redirect his anger and hit the wall. There were many holes in walls in my youth. He was very threatening, getting in our faces with his fist balled up. He called us every horrible name in the book and punished us all the time for the most ludacris, made-up shit. He took our things away and hid them all the time. Long after he died, I found two turquoise rings I had lost in the garage where he had stashed them.

He was always yelling and screaming and slamming things while drunk. I used to pretend to be asleep as he stalked over me, cursing. One time, my friend was spending the night, and he was leaning over her, cursing in her ear, calling her a whore. He thought it was me. I was probably fifteen and still very innocent in the ways of the prostitutes, yet I was always a "whore." I just said, "Dad, I'm over here. That's Diane," so that he would come threaten me and spare her. Then, in the mornings, he would be nice. He felt guilty and overcompensated. He'd make breakfast and give us hope that he was actually a great guy and that it was all just a bad night. Then, the whole scenario would repeat on a loop. I was terrified of this man and have lived so much of my life afraid of everything, all because of my rocky foundation. Like that old Bible story, my house was built on sand.

One time, while living back at home as a young adult, probably nineteen or twenty, my father came home drunk and enraged. He was chasing my mother around the kitchen table, and she was so scared. I ran up to him and told him to "fuck off and die." He ran after me and cornered me on the steps. I just stopped and told him to do it, to go ahead and hit me. I was tired of the shit he put us through, and I was not going to cower anymore; game over. He stopped with his fist up, and I stared him down, waiting for impact. Luckily, it never came. He put his fist down and went to bed. He never threatened or crossed me again.

He took off and returned to Florida for a few years, as was his pattern. He didn't come back for my wedding in 1981, he couldn't be bothered with it. So, my mother's brother, my beloved Uncle Dick (Nixon) gave me away. Love is blind. It is also deaf and dumb and cannot be reasoned with.

Years later, when I was in labor with my first child, Cory, my mother was too much of an emotional wreck to come to the hospital. However, my dad came. He stayed for seventy-two hours, scared to death, as my mother would later tell it, that I was going to die. I actually came disturbingly close. At one point, when it looked pretty damn bad, he went home and got my mother, and she came in shaking, trying to be brave. It lasted about fifteen minutes before she went back home, but he made her come just in case it was the last time she would see me, and he didn't want her to feel guilty. This was while I was in the hospital before my induction (I was admitted days before with pre-eclampsia). I was quite literally strapped to the bed with one arm, so I couldn't roll over on my side. My blood pressure was off the charts. I more than likely would have died forty years prior, but thank God for modern medicine. I had a horrible induced labor, which lasted hours, then days.

While mom was flipping out at home, my dad stayed in the waiting room, slept in a chair, and drank a lot of coffee. My whole life, I thought this man hated me. Why was he here? I remember the doctor telling my husband Tony that a dog shouldn't have to suffer the way I was suffering with this birth. It was brutal.

I was swollen from head to toe. I was not allowed to eat, only fed through an IV. I would drift in and out of reality, and I was really circling the drain. I would circle the drain two more times in my life and come out fighting again (heads up: don't take the weight loss drugs).

While hospitalized, my Aunt Deane would call every day and cheer me up. Our little inside joke was the story of *The Little Engine That Could*. She would say, "I think I can, I think I can, I think I can," and I would repeat it. Anytime I was in trouble, she would call or come over, and we would say it together for the rest of her life when things got tough. We said it a lot over the years. She gifted me the book and a little wooden toy train that goes around the Christmas tree. Our connection was very deep, and the mention of that story still makes me cry whenever it comes up in conversation, or I see it in a bookstore. My little train was lost in a flood when I lived in Hudson, Ohio. I can't stand to think about it. It broke my heart to lose something so important. Still, I think about it every Christmas when I put the tree up and say, "I think I can, I think I can," hoping she hears it and knows how much she means to me.

As I sit here today with the final edit of this book, I have learned that her daughter, Linda (my cousin), is passing away any day now. She grew up very close to my sister Sandy, having been raised together. I just helped my sister pack and sent her to Florida with her son so she could be there. It's a sad day to read this chapter, to think about the past, and to think about Linda, that first baby born out of Virginia. Circle of life.

When my dad came to see Cory after all was said and done, he was the first one there. He brought him a tiny, custom-made Chicago Bears jacket. I was shocked at the sentimentality of that. This was not my father; it was not what I knew him to be. His showing of sentiment actually made me feel awkward. My husband Tony was a rabid Chicago Bears fan, and this was my dad's way of saying he cared, only I didn't want him to care. I did not want to rethink the dynamic of my life, and I was resentful of his kindness. My reaction was so strange. It felt like he was rocking the foundation again by showing feelings or—dare I say it—love. I was kind and appreciative, but on the inside, I was freaked out by it. It felt awkward and unfamiliar, like, "You can't change it all now; it's set in stone. Let's not try to re-write that book."

One day in June of 1995, my dad was away, and mom wanted a "Cory night." So we went over, watched movies, and hung out in my mom's room. My dad worked until 9 PM, then went to play piano at the Brecksville Tavern, the bar where he had a weekly gig for many years. He wasn't expected home until after 2 AM, so I didn't think I'd have to deal with him. I expected to be gone by the time he got up for the day, but I wasn't. I avoided spending time there if he was home. He upset me just by being, and by this point, I was completely estranged from him.

That morning, he woke me up at the crack of dawn, because I had fallen asleep on the sofa with Cory. He was asking for my inhaler because his wasn't working. We both have asthma (well, I do. He's dead, so he doesn't anymore). I got up, gave him my inhaler, and watched as he sat on the steps and waited for his lungs to clear. It still wasn't working, so we called an ambulance, assuming it was an asthma attack. I woke my mom up, and we put Cory on the couch in the basement with his videos (It was probably U2's *Rattle and Hum*, actually, because he was obsessed with it).

I remember hearing the sirens and saying, "Hang in there, I can hear them. They are almost here." Then, he walked over to the couch, sat down, looked up at the ceiling in a weird and confused manner, and said, "I'm going out." Then, he died. He just died right there in front of us. I am so glad I sent Cory to another room. It was horribly traumatic.

I went downstairs, knowing he was gone. I could hear my mom crying and calling his name like she might wake him up. Why we had any love left for him, I will never know. He made our lives hell, but on some level, we still loved him, apparently. It may have been the shock of seeing someone leave the planet more than actually mourning him. He did see something. He looked up at it and he felt his body going while looking almost happily at the ceiling.

I quickly tried to get to Cory to make sure he wasn't scared by the sirens and paramedics. Suddenly, I felt my legs start to go, a slow-motion wobble, as if time was bending and morphing into something unrecognizable.

That wasn't a good morning, but it wasn't a bad morning either. It may sound cold (I have written a song about these tendencies of mine to be cold and aloof in times that required a different approach), but something in me knew the nightmare had just ended. I had emotions that were so conflicting. It didn't make sense then, and it still doesn't now. It had only been a week since I "saw" his death coming, and I was not overly surprised because I know how that works.

How can one person manipulate so many people's lives in such a way that they are enslaved to it? It's a baffling dynamic. I felt guilty for caring about him, and guilty for feeling sad that he died. I felt guilty for feeling a great sense of relief that he was gone. I felt sorry for my mom, but I felt happy for her too. I felt guilty for feeling a great sense of relief that he was gone. I felt sorry for my mom but happy for her, too. We were a mess that he made, and we were left to clean it up and figure it out. Wash, rinse, repeat.

This was the beginning of what my psychologists and therapists, over the years, have diagnosed as post traumatic stress disorder (PTSD): this life with my father, by my father, for my father. It created a way of being that was not great for a child, then a teen, then a woman.

My dad hated women; he only liked my mother because she had the body of an eleven-year-old boy. When my sister and I were on the other side of puberty, he made us feel horrible about ourselves, ashamed of our bodies. He once said that he always thought I would be small like my mom and was disappointed that I wasn't. I was so thin; I just wasn't flat-chested (I was a size eight during those days, and long into adulthood). He talked about it constantly to both my sister and I. Boobs = whore. I was called a "fat slut," and somehow, I still gave a fuck when he died (but only half a fuck. The other half was just relieved, and I admit it).

Something happened to my dad in Florida when he was there, and we never really knew the details. Essentially, he was asked to leave, I guess. Just leave the state and don't look back. It had to be bad. Can someone even get thrown out of a state? He was accused of propositioning a thirteen-year-old boy in a rest area, and that is all I know. We were outraged that someone could accuse my dad of something so vile; he acted so hurt and wronged, and we bought it.

Now, I don't dare do the research, but something just always made him look like some victim of this Florida witch hunt, and we all rallied to defend him because he was so wrongly judged. He may be awful, but that was taking it too far.

Later, I would have reason to believe he was more than likely guilty as charged. He had a dark history that included some shady dealings with Bob Crane, the actor of *Hogan's Heroes* fame. As it turns out, my father was part of Crane's porno ring business. Shoes just kept dropping; left foot, right foot, drop, drop, drop. These weren't the cute Helen shoes, these were the Mrs. Buck shoes: ugly, scary, with compression socks.

I may never disclose all of it, but I am not shocked by anything now. Nor do I completely trust anyone. I'm just not capable of total and complete trust. It's unfortunate, but it seems that the people you are 100% sure didn't do a thing absolutely did the thing.

BLOW AWAY

Written by Tracey Thomas
From the 1993 album *Standing Alone*

You got black, you got white,
What you gonna do with your life? Just fight.
You got breath, you got death,
Who's gonna say which way, which way is best?

Chorus
You better wake up, 'cause tomorrow is today.
I guess it won't make much difference anyway.
Wake up, 'cause tomorrow is today,
I guess it won't make much difference to you anyway.

You got kids, sitting alone,
Waiting for mom to come on home,
You got blood, on the hands of little ones,
Where in the hell are these kids getting guns?

Run around the willow tree, blow away, blow away,
Willow tree sees no color on me, blow away.

About Blow Away: *I wrote this song when I was in the band Persona 74. I wrote the lyrics, and the band wrote the music. That was our thing. It was written in 1993 and had a lot to do with gun violence and social injustices. Racism, sexism, all of it. I could never have foreseen that it would get as horrible, angry, and ugly as it has over the last decade. Somehow, it did. I will forever hope that humankind can do better, year after year. What is Einstein's quote about true insanity, repeating and expecting a different outcome? Yeah, that's me.*

SEVEN: MY MOTHER'S KEEPER

My mother, Helen, had repeated nervous breakdowns during my formative years (this is going to be a long one). She was undoubtedly your run-of-the-mill sixties/seventies-era mom. She smoked like a chimney, went out, drank cocktails, partied, supposedly had a wicked sense of humor, and was the center of everything she did. She loved Frank Sinatra with a burning passion. She had an eye for Italian men, and they for her. She liked to go out and "party." I hate that term but it fits here.

She had anorexia, but we didn't know that then; Helen was just the skinny one. She did eat when she was happy, and looking back, my guess is she actually had bulimia.

Before she married my father (DON'T DO IT!), she and her only sister, Elizabeth Deane (known as Aunt Deane, whom I've already mentioned a few times), came to Akron from Richlands, Virginia, in the 1940s for work and big-city shenanigans. They established a life here and were insanely popular with the club boys.

I've heard some wonderfully fun stories and I'm glad I took the time to listen. I was always interested in the stories of the lives of my older family members. My mom used to tell me how she and Deane walked (in heels, mind you) from their home on North Main Street in Akron to a bar right by the bridge (it still stands, actually, though I believe it's vacant these days) to start their evening with a couple of cocktails and some dancing. They would walk in and the men would immediately buy them drinks. They would dance for a couple of hours there and then hoof it over the bridge to another club by what is now Akron Coffee Roasters.

Once there, the men would continue to buy them drinks, and they would continue dancing the night away. Then, they would catch a ride home with some handsome fellas in the wee hours of the morning. What amazes me is, according to my mom, they never took their shoes off. God help me.

My friends used to hang out at our house until my dad got off work, and then they would flee. But all of my friends loved my mom. They always asked me about my mom and the cousins, asking, "What are they saying?" I had to translate Appalachian into Ohioan...

"Far" means "fire."
"'em" means them."
"haulrin" means "hollering."
"emmer" means "those are."

I had it down and was happy to translate for my fascinated friends. To this day, my friend Andrea refers to my mom as "Hiylin" rather than Helen because that's what it sounded like when she said her own name. "Ha, I'm Hiylin."

My roots in the mountains are deep, thick, and strong. I identify with those people and that history more than with this Ohio life. Maybe it's a soul thing? Maybe it's ancestral memory, which I find fascinating! Whatever it is, in the deepest part of my being, I'm the descendent of upper-class hillbillies who were Scotish, Irish, and English, all who descended on America's mountains to be farmers and have a simple life in the New World (for texture, I do have about seven percent African/Ghanan).

My mother lost so much of herself when she married my father. I want to go back in time and show up at the little diner on West Market Street in Akron (The Chat N Chew), sit down in her section, and say:

"Hey, heads up! This guy loves you, and his mother is about to walk in and beg you to marry him, or he will kill himself, but please don't do it!" I would do that for her even if it meant that I didn't ever exist as Tracey Thomas.

Side note: It turns out that I was never a Thomas, after all! That was my step-grandfather's name. I found my real grandfather on Ancestry.com through a DNA test. My real grandfather was actually my great uncle, David Homer Coker, husband of my grandma's sister. So, my last name, biologically speaking, was always Coker.

Apparently, my Gram had children with her sister's husband, and that is the rift that broke the Hensleys apart, sending her to Akron from Kentucky. Oy vey—the drama! Tracey Coker. WHO KNEW?

My grandmother, Delila, was afraid that my (not yet) dad was going to kill himself over the fact that this beautiful dancer/waitress wouldn't marry him. She went in and begged her, using suicide manipulation, and there you have it. At nineteen years old, my mother married both him and his temper, and that was the end of her happiness, wholly, profoundly, and forever.

Her constant companion, cohort, and sister had married by now. She was domesticating with a man twenty-five years her senior, so their party-girl days ended. My mother didn't want to work to support herself, so this seemed to be the answer. She liked my grandmother Delila quite a bit, and they would live with her in her duplex on Maple Street in Akron, across from the infamous Glendale Cemetery. I often drive by there and say a little hello to the family. It is never far from my thoughts; how pivotal that place was for my family, and there it still sits.

By the time I was fourteen years old, my mother was living in her bedroom, suffering panic attacks every hour unless she was able to sleep for short three-hour medicated bursts. She had developed extreme agoraphobia and had to have the curtains drawn during the day, so it was dark in her room, lit only by lamplight and television. She couldn't eat and would drop to ninety pounds. Then we would have to sit with her and force her to eat or drink by threatening a trip to the hospital for an IV. Milkshakes became something she could tolerate, and I believe that kept her from shrinking to nothing.

She had ritualized meals and habits. Every day at 11 AM and then again at around 4 or 5 PM, my dad or sister had to go to "the Skyway," as she called it, for meals and her twice-daily Cokes—with extra ice. We had to go everyday to get her those Cokes, and some days, that was all she took in. It became so habitual that it was just part of life. When I got my license, it was my turn, and I did all the Coke runs. By then, she had stopped cooking altogether; she never did much of that anyway.

My dad was working late into the night; he played piano at a bar in Brecksville, Ohio, after he ended his shift selling cars. They called him "The Piano Man," and he was well-known. My sister married at seventeen and was off with her two boys by then, so I was on duty for the vast majority of my teen years. Then, a few years after she married, my sister divorced and came home with my nephews, Jimmy and Bobby. She was working constantly to support them, and they stayed with us.

My mother would rarely come downstairs, let alone cook, though she had a few things she did very well: meatloaf and salmon patties. Always comfort food, but only on rare occasions. It felt like Christmas when she was well enough to come downstairs and hang out with us, although we did a lot of hanging out in her room, playing backgammon, and watching TV. It all seemed so normal to be in a dark room just hanging out with mom in bed.

My sister and her boys moved in and out through the years, and I loved it when she came home with them; they were like brothers to me. My grandmother lived with us a couple of times for little spurts, which was absolute heaven. She was the best cook on the planet. There was always something wonderful going on in the kitchen. My intense love for cooking came from her and those memories of how food could be so important. It made you feel loved. When it comes to fried chicken, none on planet Earth compares to hers. I have tried to recreate it a million times to no avail.

I believe my struggle with anorexia and food issues started then. I felt love through her food, yet it was exacerbated by my father's shame when we got our "big girl bodies." Little did I know that something that brought such joy could also bring such sorrow. I developed a wicked eating disorder in my teenage years. I also had to deal with multiple stomach ulcers, before the age of seventeen. Can you even believe that? All of this was from the fallout of a bad childhood. Part of the reason I have had such a hard time losing weight as an older woman is due to the memories of being so paralyzed by my relationship with food. I didn't want a diet to trigger that again.

Another cause is the residual from watching my mother waste away from cancer. I always associate weight loss with terminal illness and have really had a hard time shaking it off. When they came to get my mother after she passed away, they told us she weighed approximately sixty-five pounds.

To this day, I am terribly afraid of weight loss. For me to lose the forty pounds I would like to lose and, quite frankly, need to lose, I would have to have some pretty intense reprogramming to know that it didn't mean death or revisiting that wicked eating disorders that I have long since overcome. But, I keep on trying - "this is me trying." (Taylor Swift, I am not sure how you wrote my life story, but you did. You nailed it, and I

Little Miss Akron

covered "this is me trying" on my *Words Can't Save Us Now* album. I'm a sixty-five-year-old Swiftie, and proud of it.)

Eventually, my mother went on an experimental antidepressant called Nardil. It took about a year, but she was coming downstairs more often. The curtains were open in her room. The trips to the ER and her stays at Fallsview Mental Hospital were less, and it was so life-changing for us. When my mother was admitted to a mental facility, I would live with my aunt or grandmother. My father worked all the time, then was out doing God-knows-what, and my family didn't think he was fit to deal with me.

The day my mom decided to try walking to the mailbox was a huge deal. It sounds ridiculous, but it was huge. She walked to the mailbox and got the mail, and we were crying and cheering her on. My sister, grandmother, nephews, Aunt Deane, and me. You would have thought she climbed Mount Everest, and in a way, for her, she had. Once she could conquer that, she would ask to ride with me to the store and "the Skyway" together. Things were different on a large scale.

My father left us yet again shortly before the monumental mailbox moment. He was in Florida at that time, and if I remember correctly, this was that same year when he got into trouble and was banished from the Florida kingdom forevermore. It's all a little hazy shade of winter now. Every time he left, my mother would improve a bit. Hindsight and all that, right?

Soon, she was able to walk around the pool in our backyard, do laps, and count them. I say "pool," which might signify money, right? We had some for a while. A little something good happened around the age of eleven when my father quit drinking for a bit and got a stable job. That lasted approximately twelve years—the job, not the sobriety, mind you. They were eventually able to buy a house after being transient and homeless for a great deal of my childhood. At twelve, my dog Jacques and I finally had a home that wasn't the backseat of a car.

They even took into consideration the fact that I loved the house when we walked through it. I begged them to buy that one. I cried because I wanted to live there so much. I remember looking out the back window from the master bathroom, thinking, "Wow, I could live here! I could have a room and a yard!" My reaction is part of the reason they picked that house. I had a room! My best friend, who was my dog, and I finally had some roots.

As I re-read this before it goes to print, I note that when I was about fourteen, they built an upscale, luxury apartment complex at the end of our street, down at the end of Smith Hill as it is known in Akron. I wanted to live there so badly. I used to think I would one day grow up to live in those fancy apartments with the pool, big master bedrooms, and walk-in closets. We walked through them when they opened, and I always said I would be rich and live there. Well, I'm sixty-five now, and while they are no longer the fancy pants apartments they once were, it's now my home. I love it here. I knew I would be here one day, and now I am. Full circle!

My dad, when sober, was a killer salesman. He made so much money we could afford to put in a pool. I got a beautiful bedroom furniture set that I picked out myself. I went with white French provincial everything. Most importantly, they got me a record player—and records! Every birthday from then on, I wanted stuff for my room, and more records! I really loved that house, and to this day, driving by, I say hello and get slightly melancholy.

Little did I know it would be the scene of a lot of really bad shit. But it will always be the only home I ever had as a child. The house was on Smith Road in Bath Township. When it was for sale recently, I walked through it, which was probably a bad idea because it gutted me.

I got in the car, and then I just lost it. All of those memories and emotions just came flooding back, way more intense than I thought they would be. We were the first family to live there, and I remember my parents paying $44,000. I had my thirteenth birthday there weeks after moving in, and I remember my friend bringing her Paul McCartney and Wings album to the party. After that, my Donny Osmond records were shelved. I fell in love with that record, in that backyard, with my little portable record player that my sober dad bought me with his successful job. It didn't last long, but it was pretty damn normal and spectacular for me while it did.

As I mentioned, most of my friends were just my Appalachian cousins. We were the offspring of the bus people, and we spent all our weekends together. Laura, Michelle, Lisa, Kevin, Frank and Ed (twins), and Raymond. There were a lot of kids born in Akron after the bus landed, and we all hung out together. We all grew up like a big extended family, and it was really fun. Our parents would play poker, switching from house to house each weekend on a rotation, and they brought their kids along so we could play together. I loved it.

Once we had that house, everything changed for the better. Even though it was still a mess, it wasn't a mess without a place to house it. It wasn't a mess in a rest area, a home that had been broken into, or a temporary apartment where the boxes weren't even unpacked. It was a mess that was mine, and I had a room to hide in, sometimes quite literally: in the closet or under a table, in the bathtub or out in the backyard.

Sometimes my mom and I would run out of the house, rain or shine, summer or winter, hide behind the garage until the yelling and banging stopped and then we would sneak back in after my dad had passed out. I was always with my dog and my mom.

The medications my mother was taking actually caused some weight gain (early antidepressants), and she looked really great! As my Gram would say, she finally had a little meat on her bones. It was a game changer on a big scale. I got my mom back, and with that came a lot of "Cinderella" shit. I did everything, drove everywhere, and made sure she got everything she wanted and needed. It wasn't worth fighting about. I was glad she was back in the land of the living, so I was happy to be her servant (and I was most definitely her servant).

This cycle lasted all of her life. I just did it. Mom first, me last. That said, I paid for it dearly. To this day, if someone says, "Bingo," I have flashbacks. She made me take her to Bingo at least twice a week, and I couldn't just drop her off. She was too nervous to go alone, so I had to stay and play Bingo in my youth—long before anyone should be made to play Bingo. I did love cabbage and noodle night, though. Sometimes, my sister would take her, but the guilt was too intense if we said we couldn't go. While she was someone I loved and adored, saying she was manipulative would not stretch the truth much. Or at all.

A note on my mother's breakdowns: the problems came on intensely during her menopause in the summer of 1973. Women's issues were unimportant then and were not yet on the page. There were no answers for her, and on a few occasions, she was institutionalized because that's all they knew to do with her: mental facilities and medication (usually just tranquilizers to knock her out). I would really hate for this country to continue to move backwards on women's issues, but it sure does look like that is the direction we are headed.

Recently my daughter, Emma, was in class at Cleveland State University and heard a couple of young men running through the halls, laughing and yelling "your body, my choice." Apparently a young woman who was in the hall let them have it, then other women came out and applaued her. I am hoping this strong, fierce generation of millennial females stands proud and fearless, demanding change and respect. My mother's generation just had to be institutionalized, so as not to bother their husbands who were trying to make a living, so everyone could live in a Barbie world. Only, Mom Barbie was on belladonna and Valium. That's what was really in the pockets of those pink aprons.

Looking back, it was all textbook. There are now treatments available that have kept both me and my sister from the suffering she endured at the hands of this insidious genetic predisposition to panic disorder brought on by menopause.

I have a strong belief that hormonal changes can cause issues in some people that appear to be psychosis at times. It seems to me like they might very well be caused by the delicate imbalance of hormones in the female body, be it monthly or during the menopausal years. Now, they are beginning to take a closer look. They appear to be figuring it out independently, without my input. But unfortunately I have a feeling they will find another place to put the effort given new laws and restrictions concerning women's health.

It's not that my sister and I didn't suffer the same issues brought on by menopause or postpartum; we both did, but there was a treatment. We drank that Kool-Aid and it was worth it. I stayed on antidepressants for over twenty-five years, having found at the age of sixty-three that I could successfully go off them and not lose it. I am feeling things again; emotions, highs and, unfortunately, lows—but still feeling, nonetheless. It cost me forty pounds to keep the "happy pills" going for that long, but it was worth it to keep the demons away.

Women, we always get the short end of every stick. Not long ago, my son Cory and I were hanging out. He said, "I finally did it." Of course, I asked, "What did you do?" He said he finished reading the Bible in its entirety. I asked him what he thought about it all.

"God fucking hates women," he said. In the conversation that followed that revelation, we both agreed that it's really on the men who manipulated the book to fit their needs, laws, and objectives over the years. Funny how history repeats. No, it's not on God, it's on the shoulders of the men who think they are God. And unfortunately, there are many.

From left to right: My mother, Helen, Gram Hattie, and Aunt Deane, taken "down home" in Richlands, Virginia.

Oh, Virginia

Written by Tracey Thomas
From the 2020 album *My Roots Are Showing*

You are my wishing tree,
You are my pot of gold,
You are the canvas for a thousand stories I've been told.
You are my destiny,
You hold my family bones,
Deep in the soil of those mountains where they used to roam.
Oh, Virginia.

You are my sun at noon,
You are my moon at night,
You are the dream inside that fuels me when the darkness bites.
If ever I've been blessed,
It's by your loveliness,
Deep in the silence of the winter when the snows confess.
How much you mean to me,
From mountains to the sea.
Oh, Virginia.

Bridge
If I should ever fall, from these highs I fly,
I hope the burden of my burden doesn't leave me dry, Oh, Virginia.
But when they finally claim, this body and its pain,
I hope to find my broken wholeness in your arms again,
Oh, Virginia.
Oh, Virginia.
Oh, Virginia.

About Oh, Virginia: *Sometimes, a song nags at you until you give birth to it; this was one of those. I can be doing dishes or mopping floors, yet I'll have this intense urge to grab my guitar. I know every single time what that means: something needs to breathe. In this case, when I say washing dishes, I mean it literally. I recognized the very physical sensation. I went to the sofa with my guitar, paper, and pen. Twenty minutes later, I had written this song. I still have the original paper that I wrote it on. I am unsure what a muse is, but I believe in her!*

This song came out of my very soul. My love for the state of Virginia and Appalachia is profound. Most of my ancestors lived in or near Richlands, Virginia. They are buried there, some homesteads still stand, and some have fallen, but I love to go back and stand on the land that was my grandmother's farm, where she grew up, and soak in the feeling of it.

This song is possibly my favorite of my own compositions.

EIGHT:
MY ONLY SIBLING AND
SITTING ON THE MOON

My sister Sandy is ten years older than me. I was an accident, and my mother didn't hold back or sugarcoat that information. When she found out she was pregnant with me, she wanted to kill my dad. She was livid. Then she said that I was the best thing that ever happened to her.

Something about the pregnancy hormones made her feel better than she had ever felt, physically and mentally. There's that hormone theory of mine again. She would tell me that I was born to take care of her, or that I saved her.

On the other hand, my sister almost did her in with her shenanigans. My sister is the most unique person you will ever meet. She is all at once insane and brilliant. When I was about six and she was sixteen, I remember her friends coming over to squeal over Beatles albums and dance. They were so cool in their go-go boots and high hair. My sister was a fabulous dancer; she got that gene in spades, inherited from my mother and aunt. She danced on television on a local show out of Cleveland, which was patterned after *American Bandstand*. I believe it was Don Webster who hosted it. She even understudied Candy Johnson, who danced in the beach movies with Annette Funicello and Frankie Avalon.

Sandy is an amazing artist, even having pieces in galleries here and there over the years. She is the most "psychic" person I have ever encountered in my years working with the paranormal arts. As I mentioned earlier, out of all the readers working for the Psychic Friends Network, they picked her to fly to Los Angeles and do the infomercial with Dionne Warwick, who was the spokesperson. She had to go on and tell a story about one of her readings that ended up keeping someone out of harm's way. It was enough to get her the commercial gig. She hung out with Dionne and experienced all the perks of being a star for a few days. Professional hair and make-up and lovely dinners were all part of the experience. Here at home, she worked with the police department in Barberton on a murder case. She also worked a circuit of psychic fairs produced by Sandra Lee Serio, a big deal in Northeast Ohio back in the day. Her specialty was spirit guide sketches, and wow, did people come to her for those. It was a perfect combination of her skills. She would sketch the visions she saw while reading people, then give them the sketch. It's common now, but back then, she was one of the pioneers of that form of reading, and I was in awe of her talent.

My sister taught me how to hone my skills with the tarot and how to meditate, but I'm terrible at meditating. I end up wandering and thinking about what I should make for dinner, or I just fall asleep. She also taught me about protection, how to keep negative things away, and how to tap out when I picked up on things I didn't want to experience.

When I was thirteen, and Sandy was twenty-three, we were starting to get into our "family gift" and decided to get a Ouija board. She was living in a little suburb of Akron called Cuyahoga Falls. She invited me to spend the night, and though it always scared me to be away at night, I did it; it was my sister, after all. Her boys, Jimmy and Bobby, were there, only around five or six at the time.

She had recently broken up with a guy she really liked, so she wanted to ask the Ouija board if she would ever hear from him again. We presented the question to the Ouija board, and the planchette said "yes." We asked when she would hear from him, and the planchette moved to the three and then the two in speedy fashion. We asked if that meant days or weeks.

It said S... E... C... and the phone rang. It was him calling—after about thirty-two seconds. We ran out of the house with the boys, down to the gas station, and called for my parents to come and get us. They did. We were freaked out, and I've never forgotten it. We actually threw the board away.

Over the years, we would experiment with these darker energies, really flirting with them. We performed rituals in a field by my house on Smith Road. Mainly, we chanted under the full moon and threw some herbs around. I wore a black velvet cloak with a hood. I had to get the look down.

We bought more boards, threw more away, bought more cards, scared the hell out of ourselves, and threw them away too. I had a pendulum (you name it, we had all the gear), and without fail, every time I would get really into the wild side, I would give it up and get right with God, who in my young mind I had betrayed by playing with these things. This was another example of "wash, rinse, repeat" in my life. If I still had all the tarot cards I had thrown away back, it would be quite a rare collection of cards.

Eventually, my grandmother and mother would set us straight about how it was a sin, so my sister and I would bounce back and forth between God and the Devil our entire lives. For a few years, we were even taken in by the Jehovah's Witnesses. My sister was really into it, threw away everything iffy, and stopped celebrating Christmas and birthdays. Of course, I followed.

I was about seventeen when a young man from our cult/Kingdom Hall came to my door and gave me a little talk about how man and woman were supposed to marry; It was the natural way of things. His name was Mark, but that's all I remember. He flat-out proposed, and I flat-out said no. Then, I met Tony a couple of years later. I got a little punky, and they threw me out. Excommunicated, or whatever the term—they gave me the boot for my rebellious, evil ways. Disenfranchised, disemboweled, something like that. So that was fun.

I was sure the truth had been given to me on angels' wings, and I tried to save everyone around me with the good news! I lost a lot of friends (and a lot of brain cells), but I was a sucker for their culty vibe. I craved a sense of belonging and community, as did my sister, so we were easy targets. We were always looking for a place to belong, to fit in. We made ourselves seem like everyone else around us because we had no real flavor of our own. Then the music thing kicked in, and I was back to being a "bad" girl. It had its moments, but comparatively, it was probably pretty vanilla in the scheme of things.

My sister hosted this amazing meditation group for a while, and I loved it so much. She lived in these great apartments called Twin Oaks in Akron. About six of us met there each week. Many profound conversations occurred there, and many interesting characters came and went. Only three of the original six are still alive.

In 2015, my sister had a stroke. She survived it, but it was a long road back. I remember seeing her at the rehabilitation center after she was released from the hospital before she could live on her own again. It was so sad to watch her try and walk down the hall with her physical therapist. She would drag her foot behind her, and her arm was limp; she was moving, but it wasn't the same. I kept picturing her dancing, so elegant and graceful, and it made me really sad. It was quite a fight for her, physically and mentally, and it was years before she really got her life back.

My sister lived with my husband Scott and I for a few years after her stroke. In 2008, Scott and I lost the farm, so to speak. We lost our savings, house, and cars. And we almost lost our business, but thank God we didn't. We had to move, over and over: five times in two years, I believe, and we dragged my healing sister along with us. She never truly recovered her intense psychic ability. It's there, but it's not what it once was. Her stroke short-circuited that system in her brain.

She never really went back to her art, either. Her arm and hand weren't the same, so she no longer could paint. That is a huge shame, let me tell you. For years, she found solace in *World of Warcraft*, online gaming, reruns of *Frasier*, junk food, and cigarettes. After her stroke, she realized something had to change, or it was just going to be another stroke sooner or later.

It's been over a decade now, and she doesn't go out much, but she quit smoking and stopped sitting in front of the computer all day. She still watches too much television and buys craft supplies she will never use. But she is alive, and if I need to call her, I can.

The one thing about losing someone you love, I have found out the hard way, is not being able to call them. I can't call my mom anymore, I can't call Tony, I can't call Aunt Deane or my Gram. I can't call any of them, and it's just weird and hard. So many times I still think, "Oh I need to call my mom and tell her." It's a split second and then I'm like…oh. But, it still happens all these years later.

I am, however, very grateful that I can still call my whack-a-do sister and talk to her about the time she sat on the moon and looked at the earth from afar. Or the time a gray alien was walking down the middle of Smith Road in the dead of night. Don't misunderstand this because those are her adventures, her mind, and her right to believe what she needs to believe. And who knows, right?!

I know her to be gifted and wise. I also know that sometimes my certifiably paranoid schizophrenic, odd, and fabulous sister can bend it like Beckham. I know she is still just a phone call away, and for that, I am thankful. Or, as now is the case with her living with us, she is just a room away, sleeping, talking to herself, or shopping for crafts.

With my sister, Sandy, and my son Cory, circa 1990

Little Miss Akron

BLUE EYES

Written by Tracey Thomas & Ryan Humbert
From the 2012 album *Queen of Nothing*

Hey there blue eyes,
Tell me what you see tonight,
Are you gonna follow me home?
Hey there broken soul,
How about we lose control?
Over everything we think we know.

Chorus
'Cause we both know too much,
And we both need somebody's touch,
The touch of someone who believes,
Do you believe in me? Will you believe in me?

Hey there blue heart,
Lonely little work of art,
Will you dance around like that for me?
Hey there summer breeze,
Never quite what it seems,
But is there ever any other way?

Bridge
Seeing is believing,
And I'm believing what I'm seeing,
I'll see you in my dreams.
Seeing is believing,
And I'm believing what I'm seeing,
I'll see you in my dreams.

About Blue Eyes: *"Blue Eyes" is about emotional bonding and, in some sense, emotional neglect. It is about someone begging to know they matter or that someone has their back.*

Many of my songs are artistic and poetic, with no real intention of telling a story. They are a flow of words with movement and emotion. With this song, I wanted to create an abstract story so the listener could interpret it independently and get what they needed out of it.

After I wrote the lyrics, my amazing writing partner Ryan Humbert came in and saw the flaws with the structure. He has the gentlest way of guiding me off the rails and into more radio-friendly territory. After a little bit of "this should do this!" — Voila! We had a damn catchy ditty.

Ryan's band, The Shootouts, recently recorded a beautiful version of "Blue Eyes" featuring Bluegrass legend Sam Bush on mandolin and longtime Willie Nelson collaborator Mickey Raphael on harmonica.

This song gets requested every time I play live. Even if I started a death metal band, someone would still request "Blue Eyes."

NINE:
TONY, WHAT JUST HAPPENED?

My first husband, Tony, drank like a fish. He turned out to be one of the absolute worst alcoholics I have ever known to this day, and that's saying something. Tony and I had such an intense relationship; nothing was laid back or average. It was 24-7 intensity—intense love and hate. We were either all together, the two of us on the same page against the world, or we were at war with each other.

It came to a head after our son, Cory, was born. On two separate occasions, I found myself with a loaded gun in my face. The first time, he was high on Ativan and alcohol. The second, and final time, I was holding my newborn son. I stood there that second time, knowing I was about to die. I felt so horrible for that baby. It was all I could feel; this poor baby was never going to have anything, no memories, no firsts. I was so scared that I froze; everything went white, and there was a smoky, hazy film around the moment that seemed to be in slow motion. I was looking directly into the barrel of a handgun being held by someone so high and drunk they couldn't even hold it steady.

I don't remember how it was resolved. I only knew that Tony left the room and I was alive, so I walked out. I left with nothing. I left my things, took my baby, and went home to my mom. I never went back. I didn't have the courage to leave the first time when it was just me, but I had the courage of a warrior when I had a child to protect. I never looked back, but I did rack up some points in the PTSD column.

That was the beginning of my panic disorder era—the day fear became my constant companion, influencer, and demon. Tony and I were such a hot mess.

I can't believe I felt so much, but I was crazy for him. I think because the dysfunction with him was different from what I was used to, it somehow meant that it was better. Of course, it was not.

The thing about being with him, years after the sparkle faded, was that his family was my family, and I loved them all. Tony had the most stable, loving parents. I adored them. They would have homemade sit-down dinners that his mom cooked with her own hands, and sometimes, his four brothers would come in and out. It was a family dynamic that enchanted me. I hadn't experienced that much unless I visited Andrea Beckett's house as a kid.

It was hard for me to throw shade on that by bringing to the table (literally) the fact that Tony treated me horribly, ruined my self-esteem, and belittled the very thing that made me...me. I didn't want to rock that boat because family was everything to me, and it still is.

It was seven years into our marriage, after the second gun incident, that I knew I had to save myself and Cory or the three of us would end up dead, and it would be the most hideous way to end our story.

I kept in touch with Tony's mother long after his death, but not as much as I should have. I was trying to wipe all of that away, or at the very least bury it, and she was always the trigger to stirring that all up again. I think I cried every time I saw her for years. She was so special to me and still holds a place in my heart, even though she has long since passed away. Some of his brothers hated me, some didn't, and some forgave me, some didn't. I find that ironic because they should have thanked me for his extra years on this planet. I held him together like fucking Gorilla Glue. Rumor had it I was having an affair with a bandmate from my new musical project. At the time, I was not, though admittedly, I did go on to fulfill that prophecy. It wasn't worth the fight, and I stood accused before I'd even done anything wrong.

One night, while at rehearsal, someone came to the house we practiced in (the home of Unit 5 bass player Mark Jendrisak, one of my lifelong best friends) and poured cooking oil all over my friend Dave Ashley's motorcycle. I knew it was Tony. Eventually, he all but admitted it but never apologized or paid for the damage. We were just rehearsing, and I was trying to return to what I knew would heal me: music. Dave certainly didn't do anything to deserve that, nor did Mark or Rob or Seward. None of my bandmates were guilty of anything at that point.

I was so over being the center of the storm everywhere I went, and after that, I had a little break. A break in my psyche, my soul, my life. I went off a little bit and rebelled against everything and everyone except for Cory. He kept me from a lot of pain just by his existence. I could mess it all up as a wife, a co-worker, a daughter, or a friend, but I didn't want to mess up being someone's mother. I knew that feeling but wasn't about to carry that torch. I used to tell Cory, "It's you and me against the world," and it really was for quite a long time.

Tony and I had developed a pretty nice working friendship after we parted. Believe it or not, that was how we rolled after the ugliness went away. We talked on the phone a lot. He never apologized, but he became civil, and he became my friend again. Like aging in reverse, we grew better as a team, raising a child together. I forgave him and chalked it up to the drugs and alcohol.

I never let him take Cory places by himself, and I never went anywhere with him. I was afraid, and he was always drinking. He had a few drunk driving events, and he eventually wrecked his truck. It just put him over the edge. I had to help him tend to all that, and he was sad and embarrassed that this was what his life had turned into. I felt compassion for him, but he would never have unsupervised visits with Cory while I was alive. I think he understood that I was not trying to hurt him. I was trying to save him. But I couldn't, and it was never for lack of trying.

I remember him calling me one night during a period where he tried to quit drinking. He had been diagnosed with liver disease because of the alcohol. He had a scary hospital stay, and when he came home, he was going to get clean and sober. The doctor had prescribed antidepressants a couple of months before, and he stopped taking them suddenly, cold turkey. He called me and asked if I had any more of those pills the doctor had put us on (I was still taking mine) because he was feeling off. He was very depressed and having bad thoughts, so I went over immediately with a couple of beers because he begged me for them. He said he couldn't quit because he was going to kill himself if he did. That was not a great choice for me, but it felt like the lesser of two evils. I ran the beer over, he drank them, and we called the doctor. I called his brother Mike and told him Tony was not doing well and that we needed to do something. I am sure Mike came to the rescue because that is what he always did for Tony. He still does that for people he loves. Mike and Margo, his wife, are still in my life and are two of the most amazing, genuine, beautiful people I have ever known.

It wasn't long after that day that I got the call that Tony had shot himself. His suicide killed something in me, too. It took out a piece that never went back in quite the same way, and though I eventually filled it, the patchwork was shoddy. I remember dropping to the floor when I got the call that Tony had died. I felt that slow-motion feeling, and I think maybe I slid down the wall slowly, but my mother was there and said I just dropped. I remember my ears ringing. I remember asking my brother-in-law, the one who still liked me, "What do I do now?"

He just said, "I don't know, Trace."

Within an hour, Tony's mom and two of my sisters-in-law came to the house to hold me in place so I wouldn't expand into the universe like a puddle of atoms and molecules. Poor Betty, Tony's mother, came to me as strong as the wind that was now blowing me away.

Little Miss Akron

She was brave and determined and was at my side. Betty knew I wasn't a horrible person and that I had tried to make things work for years and years. She knew his demons better than anyone. We talked later, and she truly "got" me. She understood and actually loved me, and I her. I tried everything to help that man learn to love and to exist in a world he hated. I wanted to rescue him. I tried to mend him, and it was all to no avail. Looking back, that was never going to happen; it was the blind leading the blind.

For three long years after that, I just coasted. I worked at a job I hated to support my cute little apartment. It wasn't until very long after that that I began to live again. It will never go away; it won't heal, and that's just life. In my mind, it has become more of a small cage than an entire cell block.

I owe most of that to Scott Shepard, who took me on as a life partner. I also owe it to my amazing little family, and I owe it to myself for realizing that I was not to blame for it all. Guilt was three years my soulmate and kicking that relationship to the curb was the hardest thing to shake. After I shook it, I was impressed with my newfound love for myself and my ability to thrive, grow, and exist in a peaceful place. Only, I wasn't. It was all bullshit because not hating yourself and not having panic attacks hourly really isn't thriving, is it? But to me, I was killing it on the healing, but it took years. To this day I don't know if I actually healed or if I just found a place in the back of the drawer to put it.

Eventually, I found myself in the middle of this dynamic between self-hate and self-love. It wasn't easy by any means; it still isn't at times. I think getting back to my music was what made me functional again, "me being me," as I am fond of saying. Now, reflecting on my life, I see that music has always been my knight in shining armor.

Punk Rock Barbie & Ken: Tony and Tracey, circa 1980, taken by Andrea Beckett on her back patio

STAND ALONE
Written by Tracey Thomas & Matt Henterly
From the 1994 album *Standing Alone*

How many nights have you cried in your sleep?
How many times have you dropped to your knees?
I wonder, still I wonder, I wonder why?

Chorus
If you're gonna walk, take a walk in the right direction.
If you're gonna stand, stand alone.
If you're gonna walk, take a walk in the right direction.
If you're gonna stand, stand alone.

When will you bend, will you break, right in two?
When will you learn, you can't do the things you do?
I wonder, still I wonder, I wonder why?

She cannot see who to be, because you overshadow.
She cannot see who to be, because you overshadow.
I wonder, still I wonder, I wonder why?

About Stand Alone: *This is the song that broke my solo career wide open in 1994. I'd been in a band called Persona 74 with Matt and Mark Henterly and Bob Kidd. That band was fierce! We were being produced by legendary guitarist Freddie Salem (Outlaws, Godz). When the band fell apart, the album was shelved. I took some advice and finished it as a solo project. This song was written with those guys, as were many songs on the Standing Alone album. I wrote this after my first husband committed suicide; I know it's dark, but it's true, and it's emotional. I knew I was on my own, and this song came out of that. To this day, it's my most requested song.*

TEN:
EVOLVING, MUSIC AND LAS VEGAS

In sixth grade, I decided to show off my singing skills by trying out for choir. We were given a song to learn, but I didn't study it at all. There was a piano, a music teacher, and an open window to the playground. I remember thinking it was scary, and I was terrified when it was my turn. I choked. I had a lump in my throat that was just pure fear. I seized up, as I would do many times in my life when confronted with something overwhelming.

The next day, a girl in my class said she heard me try out while she was near the window. She said I was terrible and laughed at me. At that point, I knew in my heart that I could sing, but I just had to hone my craft. She was wrong, and while I was embarrassed and hurt by her nastiness, it didn't defeat me like it had other times in my life; it just made me more determined.

Around that time, my parents had broken up again, and my mother and I were living with her friends in an apartment in Ravenna, Ohio. The apartment had a playground, and I was allowed to go out and play by myself, usually just sitting on the swings. My father had given me a battery-operated transistor radio before he moved to Florida (again). I always took it with me. The station I listened to then was WHLO in Akron.

One day, while swinging by myself on the playground, listening to the radio, a song came on. It felt like I was struck by lightning right there. It hit my heart and my soul and became my first-ever favorite song. I was determined to hear it one thousand times. I remember buying the 45; I had no record player at the time, but I still wanted it. I would call the radio station and request it daily, and they would always play it. It was "The Night They Drove Old Dixie Down," and the singer was Joan Baez.

I learned every nuance and knew I could sing it; it was easy to emulate and mimic. I kept it under wraps, but I had my ammunition for the next choir audition, and I remember thinking I would show that girl how wrong she was.

My next audition came in seventh grade at Copley Middle School (my second time in seventh grade, so yay me). It involved looking at a simple piece of music and understanding how to read it, and of course, you had to sing it from the sheet. I could not comprehend written music or music theory and still can't. Yet there I was in music class, pretending to know what I was doing, pretending to read music. When the audition announcement came, it was made clear you would need to sing on the spot using the theory we had learned. Only I hadn't learned it. I sat there wondering if I could pretend I was reading it and sing it from memory. It wasn't like the auditions were overly private. You could hear them in a little room off the big choir room. By the time it was my turn, I had it memorized, so off I went.

I really liked our choir teacher at Copley. He was a nice man; I could tell he felt bad for me because I froze. I panicked, and I literally croaked through it because I had that big lump in my throat, like the one you get right before you cry really hard. I was too scared, and I failed to redeem myself. I did not make choir, cheerleading, or the final cut for the diving team. None of it. It was almost always my grades or my fear that made me an underachiever. In this case, it was a big lump in my throat, once again caused by the fear demon.

By the time I was in tenth grade, I had honed my singing skills a bit. I would practice day and night. I just sang all the time. My friends hated it when we were in the car because they would try to listen to the radio, and I would sing over it. My good friend back in the day, Bob Kidd, once said to me, "If anyone heard you sing in the car, they would never believe you could sing."

In tenth grade, some artists and bands made me feel like I could do what they did. My love for music was obsessive and ridiculous. I sang along with Linda Ronstadt, Joni Mitchell, Carol King (*Tapestry*, wow!), and Carly Simon. I also loved Heart and was inspired by them to add a rocky edge to my style. I stuck with the female vocalists because I could do what they did, and it was such a good feeling to be locked in there. I had yet to discover the artist who would make me weep the hardest and hit my soul, Billie Holiday, but that would come when it was supposed to.

The auditions for the school musical were coming up, and I would once again punish myself by auditioning. I was going to do it. I was going to show this school who they were dealing with.

I had this mad crush on a boy named Arthur. He had a band, and they played the talent shows. The girl singer in that band was Mary Jo (I am avoiding last names here because it's easier than reaching out to ask permission, I'm far too lazy for that). She was one of the insanely popular girls. I was not on her radar, but I thought she was so cool, and so was another girl, Debbi, who also sang. I wanted to be them, but alas, I was not on their level. Somehow, I thought this play would do that for me: move me up the food chain.

I wanted to sing with Arthur's band, but that was like aiming for the stars at Copley High School. They performed "Landslide" by Fleetwood Mac, and I had to sit in the audience knowing I could slay that song. But it was not to be. As the auditions for the play approached, I was a little worried about the acting part; I had never done such a thing before. I didn't even know how to handle that bit, but Andrea and I decided that you go up and read it with personality, like it's just a real-life situation you are dealing with. Okay, good enough, I can do it. I learned the song, by ear, of course, and got up there, scared as fuck (sorry, but 'hell' didn't cut it here. I was more than terrified "as hell." It was way more "as fuck"). I sang and didn't choke; I kind of pulled it off. I didn't suck at the reading, either. I was not confident, but I did it. It was probably lame, that bit, but I killed the song. In the end, I did not get the part, or any part at all. My grades were too bad, but the teacher said it was not due to my lack of ability.

The fallout from that was spectacular, however. One of the popular senior girls, who did get the lead, saw me at a football game, hanging out on Friday with Andrea, like always. Her name was Dawn. She was so pretty and so charismatic. She saw me walk by and said to her very popular friends: "THAT GIRL CAN SING," like, in all caps.

It was loud and in earnest, and my life was on the move. At that point, I decided I didn't need to get good grades; I was going to sing. I was going to make that my life and career. I didn't need or want college. No one ever told me what college was, what it was for, or how to get there. In my family, graduating was winning. I graduated, but barely, and was the first in decades to finish school in my family. It was quite a thing at home, they even threw me in the pool to celebrate. When I got my driver's license, they threw me in the pool. When I got engaged, they threw me in the pool. That's what we did when big things happened: we threw each other in the pool.

In 2019, Arthur, the cool boy from high school, reached out to me on Facebook. He wanted to know if I knew someone who could get his single on the radio. We talked for a bit, and I reached out to some people for him. He is still very talented. His song was good, and I was thrown back in time for a minute. I remember thinking it was so cool that he wanted my help.

By sixth or seventh grade, I was confident enough to sing in front of my family. I would never use my own voice, ever. My thing was mimicking. When I told them I could sing, I made them come down to the family room, where we had a fireplace with a little ledge you could sit on. I made the ledge my stage. I put a long towel on my head and sang a Cher song. I nailed it, and they laughed and loved it. My mother was shocked. I was so dead on with my Cher voice, which I still use now and again to get a very intentional laugh. Then, I ditched the towel and sang "Ben" by Michael Jackson. My mother and sister were the only ones there. It was a small show with a great audience. They both started to cry. I knew then that something was going on, and I loved it. I never thought I had the power to make someone laugh, in a good way (and not at me), but because I wanted them to, and then cry afterward. Oh, the power that surged through my veins. I felt positively supernatural.

At that point, my mom called all the relatives and cousins and told them I had this crazy gift of song. It was on! I remember singing "Paper Roses" by Marie Osmond for the cousins, and everyone was like, "OH MY GOD, YOU NEED TO SING COUNTRY MUSIC!" I never did listen to anyone. I probably should have gotten that memo earlier but alas, I was heading into the punk rock abyss, and I loved it there.

Then, I got my confidence going and became obsessed with Barbra Streisand. I was rehearsing for some audition, I'm sure, at Andrea's house, and we did "Evergreen." Larry Triola was my new piano guy and great friend from Copley High School. He and I sat down in Andrea's basement where there was a little electric piano. Her parents came down to listen. Andrea's mom, Pat, was like my other mother. She was so good to me, gave me great advice, and made the best chicken soup. She told me never to grow my hair and that I should be a sassy, short-haired lady forever. Then she told me to go straight to jail, do not pass go. Translation: "Don't go to school. Take a couple years and try this singing thing."

Little Miss Akron

Her dad said, "Wow, Andrea told me you could sing, but I had no idea you could sing like that." I remember these things because I was never sure I was anything that mattered in this world until I found music. I remember all the love, the compliments, and that feeling of being something that wasn't just nothing.

I craved this attention, and they were unknowingly creating a monster. I knew I would win the whole world over. They would say, "I knew her when." Okay, granted, It ended up being like four people, but I think a few more people have said it, maybe?

I most loved singing Barbra Streisand back then. "Evergreen" was always my go-to song of hers. I liked the feeling in my throat when the notes matched up to the record. I don't know how else to explain it but I was able to match her note for note, and I had the tone down. I just knew there was a little resonance when I matched, like when you use a guitar tuner, and it's red and wobbly, and then when you are in tune, it turns green. I could feel that in my throat. I did the Babs bit at weddings now and again, and even at a drag club once when I was older. I had a lot of fun at the Interbelt, a gay nightclub in Akron. I think, it's still a little foggy.

During all this, my Aunt Deane decided that someday I would sing with Frank Sinatra. That is another chapter, so stick around for that one. But, before the Frank episode, she was pitching me here at home. She knew a nice older couple with a son in the music business. They wanted me to meet him because he was moving and shaking in his career in Los Angeles or New York, wherever he was shaking it then, but it wasn't Akron. I went to their house, sang for them, and they were lovely. They were the Sternbergs. Their son was Liam, who went on to work with amazing artists like The Bangles, and he wrote "Walk Like an Egyptian." Per his parents' recommendation, he came to see me perform with Unit 5 at The Bank, a popular nightclub in Akron at the time. He said he would come back when we had matured a bit. He liked my voice but thought I was too shy and lacked stage presence. I did, however, have tea with his parents. Maybe coffee? Fame is fleeting.

When I was fifteen, having moved on from the fireplace mantel in my basement, I hit my first proper stage at a private party at The Fairlawn Theater. I sang "I Need You" by America and "Rhiannon" by Fleetwood Mac. Once again, Larry was my pianist. We hung out constantly back in the day. This was a "gig" set up by one of my first boyfriends, Seth Stearns. He was this super cute guy from Firestone High School and worked at the local Baskin Robbins.

He got off work one night and came outside to hang with Andrea and me, and he was flirting with me instead of Andrea, which was not the norm. He seemed to be really into me, and I thought I would die. Seth became one of the first supporters of my newfound music career. Before I was confident enough to sing in front of people, he was among the first I shared that with. He was at my house, and I said, "I think I might be able to sing." I ran down to the lower level of the house and sang loudly so he wouldn't look at me. I hadn't figured out how to be observed yet. He was so impressed at my take on "Long, Long Time" by Linda Ronstadt that he became my first adorable little manager and booked me at the Fairlawn Theater party.

So here I am, the girl who didn't make choir and never got a part in the school plays, wowing the audience. I was off and running. I was asked to sing at another party. This one was in a barn for probably 100 kids, and I repeated "Rhiannon." This time there were really important people in the audience and little did I know, they were from a super popular local band named Milestone, and they was huge in this area of Northeast Ohio. I had a wicked crush on the drummer, Jim Harris, all throughout high school. If I haven't mentioned it yet,

Little Miss Akron

I was absolutely boy-crazy. Jim worked at the infamous Skyway Drive-In, where I spent most of my youth. He was a catch and a half because those curb boys, as they were called, were a score. I never caught him but it wasn't for lack of trying.

Andrea and I used to go see Milestone, featuring the grooviest curb boy, ski team champ, and best drummer ever, Jim Harris. We weren't always old enough to get in, but we would sneak in with fake IDs or go to the outdoor shows in the summer. They were always playing somewhere. After Mark Jendrisak (the bass player from Milestone who would eventually be my Unit 5 bandmate) saw me at the barn party, he asked if I would sing some backing vocals on a few songs Milestone was recording in the studio. You would think I had just been signed by RCA or Island Records. I felt like a rock star. Damn if "Rhiannon" didn't get my ball rollin'.

Then, I also began working with another Skyway curb boy named Mike Johnson, who ran sound for Milestone. Mike would later became the guitarist in Unit 5. I was trying to put a band together and invited my work pal, Bob Ethington, to play drums. Rumor had it he was fabulous. These connections were putting me on the path to what was going to be fairly epic for me musically.

A new band called Hammer Damage played downtown at The Bank Night Club. They thought if I could sit in with them for one song, I could launch a thing locally in the very happening punk and new wave scene. I was starting to write, my music was flirting with new wave, and I had become very interested in punk rock. Andrea and I decided, as the West Akron girls we were, hot off the high school presses, that we should probably dress the part. I remember wearing a black tennis skirt, tights, knee socks, Converse "Chuck Taylors," and a satin baseball jacket. I remember because it was a look I would later repeat in photo sessions, which, in hindsight, was probably not the best idea. I had my super edgy homemade Tin Huey jacket on and I thought I was really happenin'.

We walked in the door, and my mouth dropped open. The Bank was huge. It was loud and very dark, and the people were shocking. I had never been exposed to such a dark underbelly before. Safety pins in faces, ripped clothes, and black edgy haircuts a plenty. I was also very aware of how they were dancing. It was more of a "jumping up and down" on the dance floor; it was a bit wild, and I remember thinking the whole atmosphere was very demonic. The neighborhood could not have been any sketchier at that time and I felt like I was sinning my way into oblivion. So, thanks, Gram Hattie, for that.

There were also a lot of sweaty, sweaty people. This was before I even knew what "OCD" meant, but the sweat was freaking me out. I was told I could meet with Hammer Damage's manager, Dale Machak, upstairs on the balcony. He knew I was coming and was willing to talk to me about sitting in with the band.

The first thing he said when he saw me was, "You girls from West Akron?" Later, I reminded Dale of that, and while he had forgotten, he laughed when I told him I thought it was a compliment. I was so not cool, trying to be punk and edgy. I was out of my element but really wanted to change that. I was immediately enamored with the vibe of everything. As it turned out, no one really "sits in" with Hammer Damage unless you're a legit punk rocker. And a guy. It didn't ever happen for me and Hammer Damage, on or off the stage, but I had a wicked crush on their guitarist, George Cabinass.

For a while, after my brilliant work at the Fairlawn Theater and the barn party in Peninsula, Ohio, I was in a cover band called—don't judge me—Busted (winner of the Worst Band Name Ever Award). We did Led Zeppelin, Blondie, Pat Benatar, and all the

Little Miss Akron

happy hits of the day. I was not old enough to get into the bars where we played, so I would borrow IDs from people so I could put myself on stage and bask in the love for a couple of hours a week. I never got caught, even though I never looked like anyone whose ID I borrowed.

My friend, roommate, and drummer was Dave Ashley. His sister was making waves in England with her band, Jane Aire and the Belvederes. She had some hits, married one of the Boomtown Rats, and even dated Richard Branson. Jane was as hot as fire back then, and I wanted what she had going on. I think I really felt like Busted was going to get me that. To this day, Jane is my friend, or my 'wife,' as we call each other. If you ever want an evening of stories, the two of us would not disappoint. We may confuse you, but we would not disappoint you. We had very different paths and levels of success, and yet very similar fallout.

At that time, I drank the beers, didn't do the drugs, attempted the screaming, and ended up with nodules on my vocal chords. I was about eighteen when I was told I had to stop singing—and even talking—or else I would need surgery, which could leave me unable to sing. And even if I could sing, it would not be the same voice. I stopped talking.

For over a month, I walked around with a pen and a tablet of paper. My mother knew some sign language and taught me the alphabet and some words, so the two of us were able to communicate that way. It was wicked hard to be silenced. I will never forget how frustrating that was, but it didn't keep me from having to go to Bingo.

After about eight weeks, I got clearance from the doctor. No surgery was needed, and the nodules were gone. I did not take the vocal lessons that were advised. I always felt that learning to do it differently would take away what I had learned to do on my own, so I never worked with a voice teacher. I did, however, start bitching about stage volume, and the ego of guys and their loud amps on stage. If I had to scream, I wouldn't sing. So, you can either have a lady on stage, arms crossed, refusing to continue while you play loudly, or you can have a song actually being sung. I got a reputation as being difficult, but I kept my voice. A small sacrifice.

My aunt and uncle were filthy rich, wildly successful business owners. My uncle owned E. Helman Plastics, was in Forbes magazine, and hung out with the wealthy and successful people of the world. They had been invited to Frank Sinatra's "Forty Years in Show Business," a private party at Caesars Palace, but my uncle couldn't go. The invitation was for four people. My aunt was convinced that I should sing in Vegas with some hot jazz band, performing the standards I would later embrace. At the time, though, that felt like a musical death sentence.

She accepted the invitation for her and my mom to go, and she was taking me because she wanted to introduce me to Frank's people. She planned to tell them to put me in some club in Vegas. I was a new adult at the ripe age of eighteen. Deane said I could take a friend, and for some reason, I did not pick Sandy. It has been a bone of contention ever since; this conversation always comes up. In my mind, she couldn't get off work and had no one to watch her sons. In her memory, I just picked Andrea and jilted her. We may never know how it went, but my guess is somewhere in the middle. That is just how life works. You do you, I'll do me, and we will end up in the middle.

Off to Vegas, we flew. I had never been on a plane before. I was far too emotionally damaged to do something so risky, so not safe, so reckless. Hence, the Valium I took to get through it. Andrea and I were in coach; mom and Deane were in first class, but who's complaining? I was headed

Little Miss Akron

to Vegas, where I had a suite at Caesars Palace with my bestie, and all expenses covered.

Next to me was a lovely woman with a British accent. She was older, probably my mom's age, around fifty then. That seems so young now. She asked if I hated flying, so it was clearly more apparent than intended. I said it was my first time, and as a seasoned traveler, she comforted me the entire trip. She said she was going from New York to Vegas to see her son play in a few concerts, as he was on a U.S. tour. I asked her what band he was in, and she said, "The Ian Hunter Band." I said, "Oh wonderful, who is your son?!" She said, "Ian Hunter." I never will know if it was true. I did the research and can't find anything about his "mum."

We landed in Vegas, and got a limo. God forbid Deane take a cab after so much success, post-Appalachia. We got to the hotel and to our room, and I was in another land, another time and place where my fucked-up life in Akron didn't exist. Andrea and I had a suite to ourselves; teenagers let loose. It had two floors and a spiral staircase. We found out we were directly under Frank's suite. Of course, being of unsound mind and body, we ran upstairs to check it out. I kid you not, I was going to knock on the door and say 'hey.'

We got up there, and there was a large guy in a suit with an earpiece, just like you see in the movies. He was so damn nice. We made him laugh, and he was fun. We said we were from Ohio and just wanted to meet Frank Sinatra and say hi. Andrea told him I was there to sing and get discovered. She went on and on about how amazing I was; she could really sell it! He said we couldn't just come up and knock on the door; it didn't work that way. We were cracking him up; I remember doing an impression of "Luck Be A Lady" in Frank's voice, and he liked that.

He went in and returned a few minutes later with two passes for the show. We didn't tell him we were already in boojee, invitation-only seats because of my wealthy aunt and uncle.

While we were there, we called our friend Jim Harris (my youthful crush) who had recently moved to Vegas, and, be still my heart, he wanted to hang out with us that night. I was a teenager, I was unsupervised with a shit-ton of money to spend, and we had Vegas as our oyster. Goodbye Frank Sinatra, and hello Jim Harris! Being the young, dumb, inexperienced teenage girls we were, Andrea and I blew off the concert to hang with a couple of boys.

My aunt let us go through her massive amount of "packed too many" clothes. I found a great pair of brown leather, tight-ass pants on my little dancer gymnast body (I miss that body so much. It was fun while it lasted. RIP). She also had the perfect beige cashmere sweater, a little cropped number. I was decked out; the two of us looked very Vegas chic. We tried to look old enough to drink, and I think we pulled it off because we were served everywhere from Caesars to the MGM Grand. We had the best clothes, money to burn, and a limo for the evening. It was on! To this day, it was some of the most fun I have ever had.

We were so afraid that my aunt and mom would be upset that we were choosing to pass on the show for a couple of boys from Akron. Not that it mattered; we were still going out with the boys, but luckily, they didn't care. At that point, however, my mom was reeling with anxiety after the flight and leaving home. It was a big deal for her, and she was still healing from everything, thanks to the new antidepressants. Aunt Deane, who had a wee bit of an alcohol problem, was already shit-faced and rooting for me to go get some Jim Harris because God knows they had heard about him nonstop for the last year. Turns out, Deane got too drunk to go to the concert anyway, and mom was too anxiety-ridden and had to care for my aunt (it wasn't her first rodeo with that). So we were free to blow off Frank Sinatra for a night out with some boys our own age.

We had a crazy, fun night and drank cocktails like the cocktail pros we would both become. Turns out you can take the shit show out of Akron, but you can't take Akron out of the shit show (Did that work? I don't think that worked, but I gave it a go). We were in the bar at Caesars Palace at one point when the bartender told us there was a table with a couple of men who were asking if we were prostitutes. He showed us the table, and they had money in their hands. I thought, "I WANT MY MOM!" Andrea thought, "WE SHOULD DO IT!" We didn't. I had convinced myself that they were going to kidnap us and that we'd be sex workers in a foreign country forever. Alas, we made it home safe and sound, with stories to tell forever about our Vegas adventure.

The plane landed at night. I discovered that I loved flying at night. It was magical, very unlike the trip there during the day. I didn't even need to be drugged on the way back.

When we got home, the limo dropped us off at our house on Smith Road. It was dark and locked up, so I had to crawl through the garage window to get inside. I'd been there and done that a few times. Apparently, while we were gone, my dad wrecked the place. The utilities were off, and things were broken and strewn about. He was not there but probably would be soon, so we took off. We went to Andrea's house, and her mom let us stay there for a few days. My dad was livid that my Mom left and went to Vegas without him, and he lost his mind. I was so scared he was going to come to Andrea's house and hurt us. Andrea's mom said, "no fucking way." She was not even slightly scared of him, but she was ready to call in the bomb squad if need be.

Of course, my parents worked it out after a couple of days, and we went back home, but this was a pattern; this was how I grew up. To this day, I don't really know how living in a shelter or even on the street wasn't a better option than living with my dad.

Always together: with Andrea Beckett in a photo booth at Summit Mall, circa 1974

AIN'T I A WOMAN
Written by Tracey Thomas
From the 2007 album *Ghost Town*

I've heard it said, "Time heals all wounds."
But what about people like me who don't buy what they read in the news?
Your coldness is brutal, your silence unkind.
Your failure to make me feel like I matter has battered my mind.

Chorus
And a fine mind it once was, if I say so myself,
Never the first with all of the answers,
But the last one to sell, to sell myself short.

Gravity holds me tightly and bound.
Firmly implanted with feet never leaving the ground.
Loneliness rips at the flesh and the bone,
Gnawing and weaving and winding, it turns the princess to a crone.

Bridge
But ain't I a woman? Don't I still matter?
My party dress may no longer fit and it may be tattered,
But ain't I a woman?

Never, ever gonna sell myself short.

About Ain't I a Woman: *I was reading about Sojourner Truth; her story slays me. It's hideously sad, and yet she persevered. I combined her story with my thoughts on what it means to be a woman, to be completely disregarded if you aren't pretty enough, young enough, skinny enough, smart enough. And I thought, what the hell? Look at this woman's life, hear her words, and try to fathom her pain. She turned it all into something so important to the world and women. I thought, screw it, I matter too. Women matter. So it's a bit of a political protest song about the state of things as a lady. No greater lady than Sojourner Truth.*

ELEVEN: THE AKRON SOUND AND BEYOND

Coming from Akron during the "Little Liverpool" era meant there were big expectations for the bands. The first wave, as it has been dubbed, included Devo, Chrissie Hynde, Rubber City Rebels, Tin Huey, Rachel Sweet, and Jane Aire & The Belvederes. The second wave started taking shape because the bands before us showed us the path.

Emmy Award-winning filmmaker Phil Hoffman made two documentary films on the music scene from Northeast Ohio in those days; both are wonderful. The first film was *It's Everything, and Then It's Gone*, which featured the first wave of music from Akron. I was part of the second film, *If You're Not Dead, Play*. I have held on to that notion because I am still at it. Same town, different music, different venues, same love for what I do, which I don't see changing.

My friends from the day included other bands featured in that film, Chi Pig and Hammer Damage. There were other bands I would go see if I was not working or playing out myself, like Trudee and the Trendsetters, a band of my first husband, Tony. The Action included lead guitarist/vocalist/writer Mike Purkheiser, Brother of Lux Interior of The Cramps. All of the people in the scene were friends. We hung out weekly and played music together. It was such a wildly active community and I am so thrilled I was part of it.

I am currently reading Bono's book *Surrender*. In it, he discusses Live Aid, stating that all he can think about when it comes up is his mullet and how his hair from that era embarrasses him to this day. I relate to this so much; you'll know why if you watch the film.

After my experiences in Unit 5 and some other projects that found me center stage as the stereotypical blonde lead singer, I decided that people would take me more seriously if I looked more intellectual. On top of that bad decision, I said yes to being filmed (enthusiastically) in my state of physical restructuring, after giving birth to three children after my time in Unit 5. It has haunted me ever since, and of course, as someone with a lifetime of raging eating disorder issues, it is what I focus on.

It may not be a mullet, but it may be worse. I dyed my hair dark, like... really dark. I got glasses and thought I would finally be respected for my deep intellectual attributes rather than my degree of blonde marketability, I told myself that I was firing on all the pistons. I definitely was not. I think I sounded rather together, unlike the bimbo vibe I felt was hanging over my head. In actuality, I looked like a soccer mom who needed a makeover, and now it's on film forever and ever, amen.

I've gone on to pen eight albums as a singer-songwriter, including a "best of" collection and two live jazz records. I have worked with some of my heroes from my youth, including Judy Collins and Melanie. I've played shows with The Black Keys and with lead singer Dan Auerbach solo.

I have great memories of playing with Stiv Bators of the Dead Boys, who became someone I cared about and enjoyed seeing and spending time with. He fancied me, and he wasn't exactly shy about it. He was such an odd duck. I remember hanging out one night at JB's Concert Club in Kent. The bar was closing, Unit 5 had wrapped our set, and the lights were on, probably around 2 AM. Stiv went to each table and drank the residual beer from the bottles that hadn't been cleaned up yet. He came up to me and showed me one that was full of cigarette butts. He drank that, too, and then he tried to kiss me. I laughed, then he laughed and said I had great boobs, and we went home.

Little Miss Akron

Some of the punk bands from the day that we rubbed elbows with, as they say, became very successful and noteworthy. There were a lot of interesting characters in and out of Akron at that time. As mentioned earlier, producer Liam Sternberg (The Bangles and Jane Aire & The Belvederes) came to see us. We were being scouted by a lot of potential musical suitors. Stiv got me a gig playing with a band out of Toronto called The 'B' Girls. They were doing backup vocals on the Blondie *Autoamerican* record. I was in if I wanted it, sight unseen on his recommendation to Debbie Harry, his friend.

It meant I had to leave Unit 5, leave home, and move to Toronto. I didn't have the courage to do any of those things at the time. Sometimes, I think that was my crossroads; one way this, one way that. I will never know, of course, but The 'B' Girls didn't fly either. I'm unsure if I would have changed that for all of us, but probably not.

Film producer Paul Schrader came to The Bank once when Unit 5 played. He talked to me for a bit and discussed how much like Debbie Harry I was. He had just worked with Blondie because they did the soundtrack for *American Gigolo*. I got that comparison daily. Like, every…single… day. I had a guy stop outside of The Bank once, get out of his car, and tell me I was Debbie Harry, or as he put it, "Blondie." I assured him I was not and didn't look that much like her; it was just the hair and clothes. He told me he loved me and left.

I once had an interview, all by myself without the guys in the band, with a local legend journalist from Cleveland by the name of Jane Scott. She was a career-maker and notorious for only talking to people she found interesting. You did not ask her to interview you; she found you, and you said yes. She interviewed The Beatles! She was the Barbara Walters of the music scene in Cleveland. I thought it was amazing that she wanted to talk to me alone. I felt special. She spoke the entire time about the similarities between me and Debbie Harry. She said I had to know that it was a thing. Did I do it on purpose? Was I emulating her? I was so disheartened by it all. That very interview was one of the reasons I decided to dye my hair dark and wear bad glasses in the documentary film. I wanted my own identity and to be taken seriously as a vocalist and a writer of songs, but alas. It was always either Debbie Harry because of my look or Stevie Nicks because of my voice.

I never thought I sounded like Stevie Nicks, except when singing Stevie Nicks songs and that was intentional. Whatever female artist of the day they could draw a line to, I was attached. I would never be a Patti Smith; I was always just a pop singer who thought she was a critic's darling. Now, I see I was not all that original, and it's okay. I worked with what I had and still work with what I have going on now.

I hate that there are limits to things—caps, roofs, floors, ceilings, fences. I still struggle with being bound to something that isn't even visible, but I've learned to know my place and hold my tongue to the best of my ability. Music was, and is, me being me. I am that, it is who I am, not just what I do. That thing within me makes me what I know myself to be. Without it, I'm not sure what would define my life. It would be an amputation. I would have to learn to "just be" again, from the ground up, like a baby being forced into this world not knowing shit about shit.

My musical life has always been just… my life. It was magic then, and it is magic now. I am fortunate to have that kind of longevity in my career, even if it's just here, in my hometown of Akron, playing in the bars.

I am forever reworking my craft to fit my current state of body and mind. It's never been lucrative, and it has never sustained me financially. Still, it has sustained me in the most fundamental sense of the word ever since I was sixteen when I first hit the stage at the Fairlawn Theater. Or, if my grandmother was to be believed, since birth. I have tried to stop. I have talked myself into thinking I am too old, too tired, too fat, so many times. I finally decided once and for all to just say "fuck it" and sing until I physically can't anymore, all because of the advice of a wise and lovely woman I met along the way named Judy Collins.

Thanks to my amazing and dear friend Ryan Humbert, I was so lucky to have opened for Judy at the beautiful Canton Palace Theater in Canton, Ohio on September 24, 2010. He booked that show for me, backed me up with his singing partner and our longtime friend, Emily Bates, and let me shine that night.

After our set, Judy called me backstage. She was getting ready for her set and yelled down the hall to my dressing room, "TRACEY, TRACEY, COME HERE!" I was so dumbstruck because Judy Collins was leaning out her dressing room door, calling me to her. Holy shit!

I ended up hanging with her while she did her mighty hair. She had on a slip, rushing around getting ready and asking me many questions. Where have I been? Why hadn't she heard of me? She told me she had her assistant buy all of my CDs. She even gave me a shoutout from the stage. It felt insane. My father's favorite singer, of his favorite song, fanning out over my schtick. We talked a while, and I told her I was laying low in my career, coasting because I was over fifty and facing that "aging" thing. I said it made me uncomfortable, so I just didn't play that much.

She stopped, curling iron in her hair, turned from the mirror, and looked at me with her mouth wide open. She walked over and looked me in the eye and said, "Don't let those fuckers do that to you."

And that was it. I stopped retiring, hiding, and feeling guilty for playing music. I have been at it since without a break. Someone gave Judy flowers as we walked to the stage together. She handed them to me, and told the guy, "She deserves them more." I have that picture, forever in my brain and on my computer: me and Judy, not letting the fuckers do that to us.

I also had the immense pleasure of playing with one of my early music idols, Melanie. I opened for her at The Kent Stage, in downtown Kent, Ohio, and she called me up to perform "Living Bell" with her. It was a special moment for sure. She is a lovely person; one of those people that makes you feel special just by being in the room with them. Sadly, as I review this manuscript again, I realize Melanie has passed away since I wrote this. She certainly gave me a moment I will never forget, a couple of them, actually. She was truly so sweet, down to earth, and insanely talented. Her husband Peter was a dear soul and very kind to me, always telling everyone he loved them. He has passed away as well. He really liked my husband, Scott, but who doesn't?

Because of Scott and his successful music store, Time Traveler Records, which he has run for damn near fifty years, I have met some fascinating people, like Sarah McLachlan, whom I mentioned earlier in the book.

I had a conversation backstage with one of my early influences, Stevie Nicks. We only had one backstage pass, and Scott gave it to me, knowing it would be an important moment in my story. And it was. She was sweet and chatty, and it was special in a way you can't put your finger on; her presence was different. I gave her my *Standing Alone* album, and she loved the cover photo.

I can't even remember everyone I have met, worked with, or known over the years, but it's been an exciting part of the journey. It is always exciting to be in the presence of people who seem to vibrate at a different frequency than we do. For me, one of those bands is The Numbers Band 15-60-75 from Kent, Ohio. This is a band that should have launched into the stratosphere. The talent that seeps from the pores of guitarist and lead vocalist Robert Kidney is ridiculous. He is snarky, witty, charming, and extremely intelligent. I love him to bits. The Numbers Band 15-60-75 sound fills the air, fills the room, and doesn't take any prisoners. When I played JB's down in Kent weekly with Unit 5, we would run into these older hippie guys who played upstairs. I was fascinated by them. They were the absolute coolest-looking group. Charisma is not even the word. It was more than that. "It" factor? I don't know, something.

I had such a crush on Robert Kidney. I was the punk Barbie chick from downstairs, going upstairs during breaks to catch the Numbers Band 15-60-75. There was quite a war between the upstairs and downstairs crowds. Downstairs was all punk, upstairs was all hippies. I was spit on, insulted, and mocked, but I didn't give a shit; I just wanted to watch the band. That was in 1980, and they are still playing. They are better than ever, which doesn't even seem possible. The world missed out on this one. Your loss, our gain.

Terry Hynde (yes, that Hynde's brother), Jack Kidney, and Robert Kidney are three of the most amazing musicians I've ever seen on any stage, on any planet. Robert is one of my dearest friends, and it's not lost on me that being called up to sit in on a song with them is special.

I am often asked about my favorite shows over the course of my career, and I talk about my first and forever favorite in my Unit 5 chapter coming up. My second favorite show was the night I did a tribute to the music of Billie Holiday at the Akron Civic Theater. For years before that show actually happened, my dream had been to do a night of Billie songs. I was always on the fence about it because I seemed like such an odd person to attempt it. I knew in my heart that I could do it, because she shaped and molded me along my path. I was just worried I wouldn't be received well and that it may not be cool for me to take it on. My desire won out, as it usually did in many areas of my life.

Until then, my soul had taken a backseat to my brain and its youthful desires. I had always had a few great loves: folky, singer-songwriter chicks, punk rock, and bluesy jazz standards. I had done two out of the three at that point, and I felt it was time to embrace the third part of my being with this very special evening of music that was integral to my life.

To say I connected with Billie Holiday is true, but it is more intense than just connecting. I can't put it into words, but I get her, adore her, and think we share some of the same angels and demons. It was very intimidating to take on her music, especially at such a legendary venue. I was scared to be less than and really scared to upset anyone by performing "Strange Fruit." I knew what it meant to me emotionally. It slayed me and I really wanted to perform it. That song made my whole body hurt when I sang it. It resonated with me harder than any song, and it still does. I had to do this show, I just had to, and I really hoped no one would be offended by it.

It turned out to be everything I needed and wanted it to be. I got a standing ovation and an encore (for "Strange Fruit"), and no one said anything negative. I will never forget it; the atmosphere, the audience. It was indeed a magical evening.

I still include so many Billie songs in my jazz sets. She is part of my soul, and I can't imagine what my life would have been like if I had never heard "Solitude," the first song I'd ever heard by her. It changed me, and I am better for it.

Backstage with Judy Collins at the Canton Palace Theater, September 24, 2010

WAX ON FIRE

Lyrics by Tracey Thomas
Music by Tracey Thomas & Ryan Humbert
From the 2025 album *Words Can't Save Us Now*

She had a thing for the boys in the bands,
She wore black like a shadow had a hole in her hand.
You tried to touch her, and she melted like wax on fire.
Her handrawn art had infected her skin,
The colors of the past just never sunk in.
You tried to save her but she blew away with the wind.

Chorus
Please don't pull me out, I'm not what you're about.
Why you gotta be that way?
Please don't pull me in, I'm too old to begin.
Why you gotta be that way? Be that way?

Bad things happen when her eyes are closed,
Good things happen when she needs it most.
The blind lead the blind to the altar of the holy ghost.
Nothing is nothing when it's said and done
And something in her dream has become undone,
And dreams are for the weak, and the broken hearted.

She had a love and it didn't end well,
Now there's a story that she never will tell.
Well, isn't that just older than the time?
The scars she made just to prove she's alive,
Add nothing to the story or the songs that she writes.
Someday her scars will melt like wax on fire.

About Wax on Fire: *"Wax on Fire" is the story of an aging woman trying to keep people away as she struggles to understand how to transition from youth and beauty to being invisible. It is a song for and about women who are wired to be sad and introspective. It may or may not be autobiographical.*

When I showed Ryan the first draft of the song, we couldn't quite get it across the finish line. Later, we returned to it and added a few structural chord substitutions. It changed everything, and I'm glad we went back to it. It was the last song we finished writing for the Words Can't Save Us Now album.

This song's stunning, moody acoustic guitar arrangement (and performance) was the brainchild of Brian Poston, guitarist for the Shootouts.

TWELVE: THE REASON YOU BOUGHT THIS BOOK: UNIT 5

To say that my years with Unit 5 were formative is an understatement. To say they were fun, hilarious, and wild is also an understatement.

We started as The Vapors when I was eighteen. We clicked immediately as friends and as musicians. Bob Ethington, Jr. and I worked at a local record store called Record Theater. I was the folk chick and he was the coolest person I had ever met. He was an insanely talented drummer and he had a college professor vibe, stylistically (hence the nickname Professor Bob). His dad had been a big band drummer in a band my mom worshiped back in the day called The Blue Barron Orchestra. She told all the cousins on the bus that I was working with his son. Bob had some mad writing skills. To this day, one of my favorite songs I have ever recorded is "I Can See It Now," which was written by Bob.

We all contributed to the songs in Unit 5, but some of my favorites are Bob's. "Scared Of The Dark" also became the title of our only album (another Bob song). Today, Bob is one of my husband Scott's best friends, which I find hilarious because they are so different in so many ways. Every Friday, you can find him at Scott's store, Time Traveler Records, for "idiot hour," just hanging out with Scott.

When I told Bob I wanted to start a band, we got together for a "jam session" at my cousin's barn. He agreed to join us knowing that my mad love for Linda Ronstadt may be a clash of sensibilities. Nevertheless, he showed up, and somehow, we decided to find more people and start an actual band, sans Linda covers.

Little Miss Akron

Next, we found Mike Johnson, who knew Mark Jendrisak. At that point, he started out as our soundman. Then, Paul "Augie" Teagle joined on keyboards, and we were off and running—but we had no guitarist yet. We just played as a four-piece while looking for our missing link.

Mike ended up going from our sound guy to our guitarist. He had a natural pop sensibility, and he wrote "Go Ahead and Kiss Her" and "She's No One's Girl." Mike and I had been friends since his days working at Skyway Drive-In. He called me Bambi, which was my nickname back in the day. I had huge eyes that were too big for my face, and I looked like a human/alien hybrid.

Now, as a five-piece, we were firing on all cylinders. Mark wrote one of our most requested songs, "Mental State." Augie was so instrumental, and without him, we probably would have tanked before we could even play live. He had the grit we needed. Augie wrote our most edgy punk song. To this day "New Leather Jacket" is the most requested Unit 5 song next to "Go Ahead and Kiss Her." I still have people come up to me at shows to request those. My newest band, The Crones, does indeed perform "Go Ahead and Kiss Her." I could never deliver "New Leather Jacket" and do it justice. That is all Augie, and it should remain so.

For some reason, Unit 5 came across a bit, like, clean cut? Good? Sweet? I'm unsure how or why, but someone once called us the punk version of The Osmonds. That wasn't what I was going for. I was flat-out rebelling and wanted to be recognized for it.

Mike bashed a few guitars, and we did break the drop ceiling at JB's Down Under once. I mean, we weren't really all saintly! I didn't do a lot of drugs; it just wasn't my scene (man). I drank, and I rather liked Valium now and again. I was not as nice as I am now, so I had the attitude. Bob, Mark, and Augie were not necessarily turning down the "sex, drugs, and rock-n-roll," so I have no idea why, but we were known as the good kids in the Akron music scene. Bob was in a long-term relationship (with his now wife Ricki), so he didn't do the wild shenanigans that we gravitated towards. He would want me to clear that up, I believe. But drugs and booze, schlepping people home, yeah, the rest of us did that proper punk rock business.

One of my memories of hanging with these guys was how much I loved the afterparties. There was always a party somewhere after a show that usually ended at 2 A.M. I usually rode with Mark, but most of the time we would all go. Sometimes not Bob, but the rest of us hit whatever party was happening.

One time, we ended up at an apartment somewhere. (Something in my vague memory makes me think the party was here, the apartment complex where I now live, but I may never know.) Mark and I were hanging out, and I was drinking this punch from a huge bowl in the kitchen. It was more like a kiddie pool than a bowl. Mark came over and asked me, "What are you doing?!" I didn't get the issue, and he told me the punch wasn't the usual spike; it was grain alcohol. Oops! I was plastered before I knew it. I like punch, so I drank a lot of it.

Being the good friend that he was, he said we should get me home. I thought, being all punk and shit, that I would make a notable exit, so I went out to "the patio" and jumped over the railing (so cool)! Only it wasn't a patio, it was a balcony. I remember the ground not being there, and then I was flat on my back, the wind knocked out of me, looking up at the sky. Then I saw Mark jump the railing after me, and now we are both on our backs, looking at the sky. I'm sure it was a low second floor, or we would have needed some medical intervention. We just shook it off to much applause and headed home.

The next day, I asked Mark, "Why didn't you just run down and out the door?" The answer was, "Quaaludes, man."

Another time, Punk Barbie Tracey showed them how cool she was in an incident that I still feel bad about. Miraculously, Unit 5 was the band St. Vincent-St. Mary High School (go LeBron!) picked to play a formal dance. I think the Giffels Brothers had something to do with it (nod to Louis, David, and Ralph). I wore a black leotard and tights with a cropped green t-shirt, ripped and safety-pinned back together, and no pants. I walked in, and a nun stopped me and told me I had to put some clothes on or couldn't come in. The band was freaking out because we were really looking forward to playing. Mike had some pants and a belt in his car, so I put those on, and we did the show.

On the way out, I saw the nun, my new biggest fan, and told her she needed to get laid. I was so punk rock, in it for the shock value. I still feel bad all these years later. What a disrespectful little bitch I was. At the time, I was just mad at the world, and she had pissed me off. And just so you know, I do not, nor have I ever, thought that "getting laid" was the answer to anything.

The Unit 5 *Scared of The Dark* album was released in 1981 on Clone Records and produced by Nick Nicholas of the Bizarros. We recorded it at Suma Recording Studio in Painesville, Ohio. The Michael Stanley Band was recording in the same studio during our time there, so we'd often pass like ships in the night. Nice guys. Michael and I met a few times over the years, crossed paths, and shared the bill on a few occasions. It was incredibly sad for all of Northeast Ohio when he died of cancer in 2021. He was a talented guy.

We worked hard on that record and we were so excited to be doing it. We had high hopes that a label would pick it up. Everyone told us we were a shoo-in for a recording contract, and we believed it. We met with labels in New York City and did some showcases, and nothing came of it.

I've mentioned that the record didn't capture what happened when we performed live. The live shows were it for us. We were tight and fun to watch, but it just didn't translate to the album. I can't even get my hands on one of them now. They are collectible, as is our 45 with "Gracefully and Ladylike" backed with "Decisions." That 45 recently sold for over $200 on the online music marketplace Discogs. I don't even own one. I have the cover but not the record itself. We could never have guessed that all these years later, our little band of good (not so good) kids would still be answering questions about Unit 5. Who knew?

As mentioned, I'm often asked what my favorite show of my career has been. I can say with the utmost certainty that it was with Unit 5, at The Bank, opening for Tin Huey's homecoming show after they signed with Warner Brothers Records. We were hanging in the downstairs dressing room beforehand, just us Unit 5 kids, getting ready and getting our "mood" on. I got so used to sharing a dressing room with boys. I didn't even bat an eye at it. By then, every member of Unit 5 has seen each other in our skivvies.

This would be the biggest show we had done up to that point. We were into wearing matching outfits then. We all had police uniforms, mine with a skirt. It was cheeky and fun. I was all about the fashion then.

It was time to go upstairs and hit the stage, and we liked to make an entrance. That night, we would walk in a single file line to the stage, cutting through the audience. We hadn't been upstairs since soundcheck and were unprepared for the crowd. People were everywhere, just wall to wall. It was way over capacity, and we couldn't see a clear path to the stage. When the crowd realized we were upstairs and ready to go on, they started clapping and yelling. A little sea parted, and we walked to the stage with thundering applause and folks cheering, "UNIT 5! UNIT 5!"

I immediately panicked. We looked at each other like, "What the fuck?"

Little Miss Akron

Then it was on, and we played one of the most amazing sets we had ever played. The energy from people who supported and appreciated us just put the icing on the cake, and we killed it. I will never forget that feeling of shock when we saw all the people and heard them yelling our name. I will carry that one with me forever.

At the end of the "Akron Sound" days, as mentioned in the film, all of us in Unit 5 were getting weary. The band was tired of schlepping equipment and playing late into the night in all kinds of weather.

I remember the night we called it quits. We were all comforting each other because we really felt like a family. It was like getting a divorce. We were in the early years of building our adult lives, getting "real" jobs, and moving on. I still feel we should have done it differently; maybe a trial separation rather than divorce. I think Unit 5 had one more record that was never birthed. We may have retired the project a little prematurely, but we were worn out completely.

After Unit 5 broke up, Mark, Bob, Augie, and I started a project called Gone To Egypt. We wrote some pretty great songs, played out a couple of times, and it showed the potential we had to carry on. We did not, and I think that's okay too.

There are so many people from that 1979-1982 era of the Northeast Ohio music scene with whom I still socialize. It was a family vibe and put me on the road to what I would, unknowingly at the time, do with the rest of my life.

Looking back, I realize Unit 5 was the pinnacle. It was the absolute most fun and the foundation for everything I took on after. I'm always asked about the band, the music, and the experiences. These are just a few things I thought I would share, so here's to Bob, Mark, Mike, and Augie. Love you guys forever and ever, amen.

Unit 5, then and now. From left to right: Mark Jendrisak, Bob Ethington, Tracey Thomas, Mike Johnson, and Paul 'Augie" Teagle

QUEEN OF NOTHING
Written by Tracey Thomas
From the 2012 album *Queen of Nothing*

The past is gone, and the future does not yet exist.
I can't relate to my present state,
What kind of screwed-up joke is this?
Wine and women, men and dancing,
Wars for reasons no longer withstanding.

Chorus
I used to be the Queen,
The Queen of everything,
People brought me presents,
Then they dropped down to their knees
but now, I'm a peasant, it isn't pleasant,
In this messed-up state of things.

Mary Mary, quite contrary,
Not what you could call ordinary.
Cousin Elizabeth wanted me cold and dead.
I meant to do her in, but she got me instead.

Bridge
In my dreams, I'm wrapped in ermen, sitting by the fire,
I am still the one, that they all love, I'm still filled with desire.
But when I wake, I have to face,
That I am now the queen of nothing.
Nothing much.

About Queen of Nothing: *I am obsessed with British history and the monarchy. Before Virginia, my people were mainly from the British Isles. The majority of my DNA is that business.*

I love author Philippa Gregory. I was reading The Red Queen and started thinking about how fun it would be to write a song about the dynamic between Queen Elizabeth and Mary Queen of Scots.

I did that and added a twist: it's also me, here and now, Tracey from Unit 5. Then and when. It's all at once about both subjects. Think of it as "fusion" in a food sense, Italian and French or Japanese and Greek, all presented as one cohesive dish. I'm pretty damn bad at cooking fusion dishes. Still, I think I can write "fusion" because this one turned out to be something I was not afraid to present to the public, unlike the fusion dishes I have made.

THIRTEEN:
MORE OUT-OF-ORDER RAMBLINGS OF THE UTMOST IMPORTANCE

When Tony died, I surrendered, waved my white flag, and hid in the trenches. During that time, I firmly decided that I never wanted to be partnered with anyone again. I was always a commitment-phobe; it didn't matter if it was work or love life. I wouldn't stick with it if it meant I had to act a certain way and that someone else's opinion of it would matter. I was out. I lasted over seven years with Tony, which was record-breaking for me.

I have had more jobs than I can count throughout my life, only to quit within one or two months. I have dated so many wonderful people, but as soon as it turned into "be my only person," I broke up with them. I would panic when I felt like something was becoming a real thing in my life. I am ridiculously changeable, spontaneous, and impulsive. I blow with the wind as if I am the wind itself. There is a movie with Juliette Binoche called *Chocolat*, and I have never felt so much like a character in a film. I always go back to watch it repeatedly, finding new things to relate to. It is just a "B" flick, but it's my "A+" flick.

Over the years, I have started businesses, then bailed. My sister and I once had a bakery together. It was a great spot, and we had some local traffic, but we both freaked out and sold it. I cost Scott an arm and a leg with that endeavor.

I have been a managing cosmetologist, a waitress, a line cook, a fast-food worker, a secretary at an elementary school, a baker, a retail goddess, a makeup artist, a tarot reader, a tarot teacher, a volunteer, a certified florist, a hostess, a musician, a telemarketer, and a lifeguard. There are likely more things I have long since forgotten, but the pattern is obvious. I start, I quit.

I often wonder if it's because I was so moveable as a child growing up. Some therapists agree, and some say it's deeper than that, but moving thirty times before the age of twelve was probably a factor.

I bring this all up in this chapter to convey how important my life as a mother and a wife has become and how committed I am to this dynamic. I have been married to Scott Shepard for thirty years, and neither of us has taken that lightly. We fight for it; we are a team and are better together than we are on our own. I'm difficult, he's brave, and it works.

Once I had children, nothing else was even a close second. I was all in, and I still am. Something about having the ability to shape and mold a family, bring it together, and make it special has cured something in me. My wanderlust is not the same; it is not gone but has priorities now. My kids (now grown adults) and granddaughters come first, period. I have committed so wholeheartedly to this that it shocks even me. I didn't bail, I didn't run, I didn't freeze up. At this point, I more than likely won't. I took to this "mothering" thing like a duck to water.

I also have to pat myself on the back for not bailing on my mother throughout her lifetime, as dicey as that was. I was her rock, and she called me her savior. Though I had moments when I needed a minute to breathe and hide from it, I always returned and resumed the work. I was her caretaker through her horrible years with panic disorder and agoraphobia; we all were at some point—my sister, father, even my nephews Jimmy and Bobby. For some reason, I was the one who could be relied upon in this situation, and that has become more important to me as I grow older. I know instinctively what is an absolute "must-do" and what can be cast aside for a bit, and it has served me well.

I have had so many wonderful friends; some have fallen away, some have gone on to whatever lies ahead, and some are still here. For that, I am grateful.

In 2023, I started a band called The Crones. We are five women over the age of sixty. When the Covid-19 pandemic hit, and I was thinking about things I had never gotten to do in my life, it came to me to try this. I was sure Covid was going to kill me. On the other side of quarantine, finding myself still on the planet, I made it happen, and now here we are. An idea manifested. The band performs only female-fronted hit songs from the eighties. it's a brand, it's what we do, and it is so much fun. We have people walking through the door with canes, but their spirit is timeless, ready to relive our youth together, even just for an hour or two. Of course, most of us can still kick up our heels and come in unassisted, but the point is, The Crones and I are pulling them out to live a little more than they were. It's more than I thought it would be and means more to me than I thought it might.

It turns out it isn't just me doing it for myself; there was a need and a void—for older women predominantly—and we filled it a bit. The band features Linda Harrison Millar on bass, Amy Walker on guitar, Nancy Rogers Peters on drums, Melissa Ulrich on keyboards, and me on vocals and some guitar. I have found a sisterhood here that was unexpected. We support each other, laugh, go to movies, and go out for cocktails. When I say that it's precisely what I needed at the exact time I needed it, I am not exaggerating or making it more important than it is. It's just the truth.

In the summer of 2023, my husband Scott was diagnosed with congestive heart failure, and a severe case of it. We all thought he was going to die, and it wouldn't be long. The heart shock treatments didn't work, and the meds helped, but they had demons of their own to possess him. It was so scary that I don't even remember it all. It's foggy, blurry, blocked out, stuffed away where I am happy to leave it, with all the other stuff I don't want to deal with. Most fortunately, a procedure in September of that year has put him back on track after six months of "what the hell is happening?" He can live a little again, though the pace is a bit slower than it was; he is alive and functional and still going to his true love, Time Traveler Records, daily. He could not work for quite a while, couldn't drive, and didn't know what the future would hold if there were even one. Our friends and our city contributed to an online GoFundMe account that saved us from losing everything.

This city loves Scott and has shown it before when there was a break-in at his store. We lost $10,000 worth of merchandise and cash, and a GoFundMe saved the store. To say my husband is a beloved human in Akron is not a lie. All the acts of kindness during this horrible season of doom lifted his spirit.

I was so tortured when this went down. I packed up our house and said we had to go. I got an apartment in a different place, trying to escape everything, rip it all up, and start over. I was, thank the Lord above, loved, advised, and redirected back into sanity by my husband and my children. I took a breath, listened to them, and got the help I needed to deal without fleeing and we stayed in our house for a bit. Ironically, once I unpacked it all again and decided to root to the best of my ability, our landlord sold the house. We really loved it there, we wanted to buy it and we asked him how much. He gave us a price that was not doable so we packed again and moved. I recently found out that he sold the house for $50,000 less than he originally quoted me, a price we could have easily afforded. I just had to trust that the universe wanted me to mosey along...again.

So much of my reality check, which consisted of finding joy in yet another mess, was because of this band of women, my music-making Crones sisterhood. Right as we started getting the Crones ball rolling, our drummer, Nancy, discovered her husband passed out on the floor, unresponsive. Her husband had a brain ailment rather like a stroke or an aneurysm. He was in the hospital and then rehab, unable to live the life he once lived. He's now in a wheelchair and doing so much better, but their way of living has most definitely changed. We had the same thing to deal with in our lives, and somehow, the universe put us together to experience it and to lean on each other.

During the second week of rehearsals, our guitarist, Amy, lost her mother. It was sudden, unexpected, and terrible. A huge blow, and yet she soldiered through it, still caring for her father on the other side of it. Soon after that, our bass player, Linda, had a health issue with her husband and had to do some rethinking about her life moving forward.

We were freaking out, thinking that our Crones project was cursed. I realized that we were not cursed; we were blessed more than anything. We seem to have come into each other's lives when we most needed friends and sisters to lean on. Looking back, it was kind of cosmic. I don't believe it was an accident, and it doesn't feel like a coincidence. It feels like someone has my back, and I love every minute of it. The Crones project is so much more than a band, and we are taking it a day at a time, trying to relax and have fun. There is a lot of talk about things like: How many steps to the stage? Do we have anyone to carry our stuff? A lot of talk about how bad our bodies hurt after a two-set night. We just laugh, and laugh. Sometimes we cry but mostly, we laugh. We go out together, we hang out at each other's houses, and our husbands have become friends. It's special.

Women in music are always underestimated. It all seems possible when you are young, marketable, and looking at the world with the power that stage of life gives you. Yet, they still reign you in, making sure you know your role and your worth—the way they see it. You start to round the corner into "less marketable" as the clock ticks. At the same time, your musical skill and talents are growing, but your ticket sales are tanking.

Then it's a conundrum. In my case, I was honing my skills when I hit the age of forty, and physically I felt like I was sledding down the hill at lightning speed. People were more concerned about the shape of my body than the music I was creating, and they didn't mind telling me. That's when I started to mourn the music career that I loved more than anything. I mourned the loss of it because I felt like all the ships had sailed, all the lights had dimmed because I failed to stay young and sexy.

Then, I began seeing women that I found to be beautiful, talented, and inspiring all over the place, saying, "screw this." Judy Collins, Chrissie Hynde, Stevie Nicks, Lucinda Williams, on and on the list goes. I'm not sure why, but aging rock star men are more accepted, sell more tickets, and get more love than women in this business. That's actually the case in most businesses, which always gets my goat. I never understood what "getting the goat" meant, but someone is always taking our goats. Okay, I'll let that go now.

I've learned through this experience that women seem to stay true to female artists more than men do. Our audience is eighty percent women of a certain age, and damn if it isn't brilliant. We have some wonderful men who come out and support us, but most of our audience is women, the old punks, and the new-wave chicks who wore crucifixes and spandex in the eighties.

The five of us agree it's not time to go to pasture when you can still bring the goods. If people don't want to watch us do our thing because we don't look like twenty-year-old supermodels, they don't have to come. But for now, the last laugh is ours. Some fierce women want a reason to dance the night away, and we've got them covered!

Something cool happened at a recent Crones show. A woman came up to me and she was all misty and tearing up. She grabbed my hands, looked me right in the eye, and said, "Thank you." I said, "For what?" She told me that there was nothing out there for her and her friends, and that we were representing and performing the music she loved and knew from her youth. Then she thanked me again and walked away. It happens at almost every show. I got choked up, too, because I know how she feels. I know how we all feel about being invisible in this world. Crones, indeed.

The Crones: girls still wanna have fun. Back row: Tracey Thomas, Melissa Ulrich, Nancy Rogers Peters. Front row: Amy Walker, Linda Harrison Millar

WORDS CAN'T SAVE US NOW
Written by Tracey Thomas & Ryan Humbert
From the 2025 album *Words Can't Save Us Now*

We danced around the table, kind of pretty but kind of drunk.
Trying to keep the world at bay, until we open up the trunk.
It fits me like a glove, the life we're kind of living,
But enough is not enough,
When you don't know what you're giving away

The moon closed in like a shadow, breathing down my neck.
We scream "it doesn't matter," but I've got no voice left.
The storm clouds spit the lightning, and the wind sings out my name.
When you don't know what you're giving,
You can give yourself away.

Chorus
I held the book so tightly, that I bent it all to hell.
The water's in the white house and the baby's in the well.
I tried to talk above you, but you never would shut up
And now we'll never know, how much is just enough.
'Cause words, words can't save us now.

The devils rule the big house, and the angels fell asleep,
I want to run too far too fast; so I'm heading for the keep.
I'm lost and no one's looking, lost and no one knows,
It's hard to hide your feelings, when they still exist in prose.

Will the demons slay the angels, and are angels even real?
Do you think about the hand of God erasing all you feel?
Will the flood wash out the sinners who are beggin' for a deal?
Do you think about the wrath of God every time you steal?
And lie, live, and die?

About Words Can't Save Us Now: *It's unusual to be sure, but it does happen. I had a dream, and in the dream, I heard someone say, "The water's in the White House, and the baby's in the well." I woke up and said it into my recorder. It's always nearby in case this happens (OMG, if anyone ever listens to some of this crazy shit).*

I couldn't figure it out, but liked the imagery and idea. Well, I didn't "like" that a baby was in a well, but I figured it must be symbolic. I grabbed my guitar and wrote the song the next day. I have dreamt a lot of lines and ideas for songs. Sometimes they work, and sometimes they don't. I think this one turned out pretty darn cool.

I used to play it a little differently. The original structure was different, until my musical brother and co-writer Ryan Humbert and I rearranged it while looking for songs that might work for an all acoustic album. He suggested making one of the verses the chorus, which completely woke the song up.

It's political, Biblical, and apocalyptic, and I liked it enough to make it the album title, too.

FOURTEEN: THE DEMONS WE SLAY AND THE DEMONS THAT STAY

Health is health; it shouldn't be categorized above or below the neck. If you are well, you are well. If you are sick, you are sick. The women in my family have struggled with mental health issues as far back as stories go. It is genetic, and in my humble, uneducated opinion, it is often hormonal. Sometimes, it is just life, and I don't always have all the tools in my box. I mean, I have the basic tools, but some of the special stuff that the best handy folk have, I don't have. I'm missing a couple drill bits or something.

I have had four nervous breakdowns during my time on this planet. One was due to severe postpartum depression, and the other three were due to my lack of drill bits.

During the last episode, I left the house alone at night, freezing cold in the icy rain. I walked from my sister-in-law's house in North Hill to the hospital in Cuyahoga Falls. I had no socks on and I was frozen when I got there. I went to the ER and asked if someone could please help me. I was in a haze, I was faint, I was not thinking clearly, and I needed some help. They told me they did not have anyone to help with psychiatric issues, which I readily admitted was why I was there.

They called Scott to come get me, gave me a mild tranquilizer, and sent me home. I was unwell for weeks after that. I was so triggered, so raw, and in pain. I shook, was freezing, and couldn't get warm, which still happens when I have emotional episodes. I was not eating much and not thinking clearly. I slept a lot, I sat a lot, and I played video games. I did nothing worthwhile. I didn't go back to work.

I quit my job (I am so sorry, Jill. I love you). I was a blob of molecules trying to reshape themselves into something useful.

It takes weeks to shake one of those grand mal breaks, maybe more than weeks. As I write this today, I saw the news story about a famous Hollywood actress being institutionalized again after being found naked and alone walking around in LA. My heart broke for her. I understand that kind of pain and that feeling of knowing you are breaking and unable to stop it from spiraling.

After all that illness, I got all I needed to recover fully from my family. My family loves me in the most amazing way. Scott and I pick and piss at each other. Cory rolls over me with his intensity sometimes. My daughter Emma and I get into it more than we should, and because we are similar, there isn't a lot of calmness in some of our discussions. My daughter Marisa always thinks there are meanings behind my words that aren't there. All of that usual bullshit that families do to each other exists in ours as well. What also exists in ours is this sense of overcoming and perseverance.

Another time I had a breakdown was after the stress of losing everything in 2008. I loved my house so much. Given my past, you can imagine how much a home meant to me. We lived in an upscale community for eleven years; we ate at Russo's, my favorite restaurant to this day. Scott and Dave Russo were pals; they swapped food for records or concert tickets. It was a great deal for us!

My job was to keep the home fires burning, and I loved it. I did not see the crash coming. I thought I would be in that house, on that land, in that community, forever.

When I was young, I always thought I would end up in a fantastic little studio apartment in New York, playing in bands and living in the city.

My friend Patty Donahue (The Waitresses) had such an odd and unique place there and I wanted the exact same thing that she had going on, even though her bathtub was in the kitchen. Surprisingly to me and everyone else, I ended up loving being a domestic goddess. I embraced traditional roles, and I was a walking stereotype. I loved it, and I still do. I took care of the house, the land, the kids, the pets, and my mother. She lived seven years with us, well past her expiration date, and it floored her doctors. As always, I was my mother's keeper. It was nice having her there, and I felt like I could control her outcome. I couldn't of course, but I tried. We fought a lot, but we loved a lot too.

Having said that, there were times when I would go into the bathroom, lock the door, turn on the shower, sit in there, and cry with a glass of wine. The kids would knock on the door, saying, "What are you doing? Can you make me something to eat now? Are you still crying?" The dogs would bark, and my mom would ask for something she could easily get herself. God bless her.

The lawn needed to be mowed, the dishes needed to be done, and the noise wouldn't stop, and yet, I did it. I committed despite how hard that was for me. I cried a lot, but I didn't really break as hard as I could have during that time, which proved to me that I had more to work with than I gave myself credit for. I cry when I am overwhelmed more than I cry from being sad. It's a response to stress for me.

When we lived in Hudson, Ohio, my favorite thing was mowing the lawn. It was something I had never known before then. There was a peace about it, and I miss it to this day. I would ride around on my brand-spanking-new John Deere riding mower. I was meticulous about the lines and the cut of the grass. I would sing, ride my tractor, and breathe in the air, which was fantastic because our house was so remote. It was a one-lane road, a dead-end. Our house made a wonderful home, and I still mourn its loss.

At times, being responsible for everyone's everything was incredibly overwhelming, but it was also rewarding. I am not sure I ever felt I was doing something worthwhile with my time until living in Hudson. Raising the kids, caring for mom, and having my own home, which I loved and decorated, and redecorated again. I was in the midst of utter chaos at times, but I was very at peace with it.

I drove the kids to school because they could, of course, be kidnapped walking to the bus. If they did take the bus, I would walk them to the bus stop. We ended up, every one of us, hating to get up half an hour earlier to catch the bus, so I just drove.

The winters were awful; driving in the winter, clearing snow from the windshield before the sun came up, but it was very much worth it to sleep that extra half hour. Besides, if I dropped them off and obsessively watched them as they went into the building, it was far less likely they would be kidnapped or killed. I was so overprotective, like my mother before me, that I couldn't even relax while they were in school for fear something terrible would happen.

We talk about it today; how fearful and hyper-diligent I was. I know it was smothering because I was raised like that by a mother who worried constantly. I just couldn't get the thoughts out of my head, and I made a lot of mistakes with my children to quiet those thoughts. I was worried every minute, I'm still worried most minutes, just not "every" now. I was trying far too hard to undo a pattern I did not have the correct tools to undo. I thought it would rewrite history if I loved them a ridiculous amount and was overly involved and affectionate.

It actually did make a difference. Those practices created a new dynamic but masked the old one I wasn't exactly rid of, but had buried most completely. Like my mother, I was still very emotional in the presence of my children. I didn't even realize it was not a good way to be. They did not need to know that side of me when they were young, and I feel terrible that I was not aware of the abnormality of it at the time. I do now and keep it in check when the granddaughters visit. Live and learn, and all that.

I also failed to structure. I didn't have a routine because it was alien to me. I never had a bedtime, a homework time, or a schedule. I fought with Scott so much about this. I thought it was no big deal to let them go to bed on their own time and do the work they had to do when they felt like it, all loosey-goosey. That worked for Cory, more than the girls, because he was wired like me. I thought a less structured life would be better for him. He thinks I was wrong, I think I was half wrong.

Marisa struggled the most from my flex; she needed a routine and more structure than I provided. Emma and I struggled the most in our dynamic because I would butt heads with her, show emotion, and react. We pushed each other's buttons from the beginning.

I have learned so much over the years, thanks to the experience of raising these three amazing humans. I have learned what not to do, which may be more important to new parents than learning what to do. The old saying that "regrets are a wasted effort" gets thrown around a lot, but I am not sure I agree. Regrets make you rethink things and do them differently, but you can also waste a lot of time looking backward. I stopped that long ago, until I decided to write a book, so, thank God for a good red wine, dry and full bodied.

The only thing I can do is to be present now. I try to live in that space truly, without looking back and certainly not looking to an undefined future. One of my absolute favorite books is *Be Here Now* by Eckhart Tolle. I have gifted it to people and I have read it like a bible. I believe that is why it has been difficult for me to write this. I am looking back and it is a series of reactions based on things I had long since shoved away.

My relationship with Scott has been a miracle. After Tony died, I didn't even have a date for three years. I was trying to recover from another breakdown caused by the shock and grief. I kept it in check with help from my mother and sister. Sometimes they would take Cory overnight to give me time to "not be anything." It helped, and it healed me to have those times to grieve, stay in bed, not function, and absorb this new life that I never asked for.

When Cory was with me, I was on. I never wanted him to suffer any more than he already had. He had a bad start to life on this planet, and I would fix that no matter how much strength it took (and it took a lot).

Scott was a guy I knew from our Unit 5 shows. It seemed like he was there every time we played. I used to call him "Nick Nolte" because he looked so much like him. He told me once he waited for me because he had a feeling I was his person. I was married to Tony for seven years, and while he wasn't exactly "not dating" during that time, he maintained the feeling that we would be together. There you have it. I was now divorced, three years single, off the grid, and he reappeared in my life because of an Elvis Presley album.

Cory went through an Elvis phase. He was six years old and wanted an Elvis album, the one where he was wearing the white jumpsuit on the cover (*Aloha From Hawaii*, I believe). I, of course, took him to Time Traveler, the local record store (and the best record store ever). I was standing in the Elvis section, a kid in tow. I looked behind the counter, and I just knew. I even thought, "OH GOD, no, I don't want to go there." I had a little talk with God right there in the record store.

I did not want to partner with anyone, never, ever again. I would raise my son, have a garden, meditate, or, let's be honest, fall asleep, and live a reclusive life. I just had a strong feeling in that moment, that Scott would change that plan, and the rest is, as they say, history.

I caved, we married, had two more children (my incredible daughters Emma and Marisa), and we have been together thirty years.

I don't know how he stuck it out during our first few years. I was such a mess, and I didn't even know it. He is solid, stable, reliable, kind, honest, and hilarious. Everyone thinks he is hilarious. I am just annoyed with all the dad jokes at this point. But the kids, they crack up at everything, I roll my eyes, and that's our shtick. He deserves a medal of some sort. Or at the very least, a trophy. Our children adore him. They love him in such a lovely, honest, simple way. I picked the right guy for the job. I was determined to do that if I ever partnered up again. That whole "while you are making plans, the universe has other plans," or whatever the hell that saying is, seems accurate. Scott was not in my plan and yet here we are.

After living three years single without any outside influences, just Cory and I, alone in the world, it was a hard decision to partner up. For the first time, I had found myself in control of my life, with some money to sustain us, some jobs here and there that I never liked. No one in my enviroment was fighting, throwing things, yelling, abusing, or living in fear. It was peaceful, even happy.

Those three years were amazing and healing. I still had to tend to my mother, which meant driving back and forth from my apartment to her place, still on Smith Road, where she lived alone for a while. It was remarkable, really. Postmenopausal Helen was pretty solid. Eventually, my father was back in the house, and they had a pretty quiet, run-of-the-mill relationship in their old age. After all was said and done, they were friends and content being together.

I remember going home for a visit. Cory was probably five, Tony was gone, I was mending my life. My father was out working on the pool we had installed when he was sober and successful. He was lying on the ground, cleaning out the filter so he could continue sweeping. It hit me over the head, like a wave of nausea, actually. I knew he was going to die. I said to myself, "Remember this moment, take it in, all of it," and I did. He wore a pale green and white striped, short-sleeved button-down shirt, with ugly brown polyester pants and his ugly Mrs. Buck style, gray shoes. I remembered all of it. Within a week, he died.

That is how my visions work. There is no precursor; they appear out of nowhere, sometimes with a bit of nausea, and then they are gone. I told my mother to prepare herself, and she did. She thought about some things and acted accordingly. We all knew that if I had a vision, most of the time it became a real thing.

This has been hard for me, to fess up about having some mental health issues. It is embarrassing at its core, really. But to sit and write about yourself is embarrassing overall. Because this "record of my life" is mainly for the generations that come after me, the blood of my blood. I think it needs to be discussed, just in case they carry the same burdens in their own lives.

My guess is that by the time you walk this world—if we don't destroy it before you have the opportunity—you will have even more tools in your box than I did, and I hope that you will find some comfort in knowing it's just how we are wired, and it can be dealt with. For anyone, my people or not my people, there is always a way to re-wire and re-write. And I truly believe that.

With Cory, circa 1992

COLD

Written by Tracey Thomas
From the 2020 album *My Roots Are Showing*

Too many secrets have burned a hole between us.
We keep trying to stomp it out, but it just makes more smoke.
Tomorrow's a new day, if you can get through today.
Somebody said that, but who is this somebody anyway?

Chorus
And I have no fear of jumping right to it.
Let's say all that we know to be true.
If you don't lie to me, then I won't lie to you.
Is it asking too much? I'm not asking too much.
Winter is coming, soon the fire will be humming.
Just like an old friend that I miss so much.
I don't like the sun, and I've never been too sentimental.
Does that make me cold, baby?
Does that make me cold?

Bridge
When does it heal?
When do we yell and scream?
I've spent my whole life holding everyone together.
What am I holding in place so hard it makes my hands bleed.
Like nails to a cross or a slap on the face,
Am I being cold?
Does that make me cold?
Am I being cold?
Does that make me cold?

About Cold: *I wrote this when I was living in Madison, Ohio, on gorgeous Lake Erie, with my lifelong friend Janie, who was ill. Sitting by the lake with a glass of wine, I had a fire in the pit and reflected on my life. I had moved up there from Akron to help care for her because her husband had just died. I left my life and my husband (I thought it was okay to only see him on the weekends) to live in this mansion on the lake with my friend. I knew all along that what I was really doing was running away again, as I do.*

I like to say this song came right out of the lake and spoke to me. I went home eventually, realizing maybe, just maybe, I really am a cold fish.

FIFTEEN:
MEMORIES OF A WICKED STORM

My sister and her husband, Terry Walker, founding member of the band The Bizarros, moved back from their wonderful condo on the ocean in North Carolina to be closer to family. They came up when my father died, and it made them realize home is here in Akron, with family, friends, winters, and all.

We discussed it so much, "What should we do with our mom?" "Would she be okay?" "Could she keep the house?" My mother eventually ended up with both my sister and me, off and on, back and forth.

The house on Smith Road was lost because my evil uncle took everything away after my Aunt Deane died. He booted my mom out of her home, the one Deane bought her after my father passed away. She told my mom that would be her home and she would never have to worry again about being displaced. My uncle had turned into a horrible human being after he became wealthier than 90% of the population. He used to shoot off his gun in the house just to scare my aunt. This once humble little shoe salesman ended up making millions of dollars and turning into someone no one recognized anymore. Money changes people, and not for the better in many cases; this was one of those cases.

After my aunt passed away, he handed me a check for $10,000, knowing that I was signing up for assistance after leaving Tony and I was figuring out my life. The check was mine if I would move in with him and be his person. Remember now, this man was my uncle, the husband of my second mother figure, my beloved Aunt Deane. I have pictures of me at age two with him. He was my funny, adorable Uncle Jerry. We spent all the holidays together for my entire upbringing. He eventually became fabulously wealthy due to my Aunt Deane encouraging him to invest in plastics. As I have mentioned earlier in my Vegas adventure chapter, he had become a mover and a shaker—and a giant asshat too.

He put his stepdaughter (my cousin Linda) and her husband on a hit list. He propositioned every single woman in the family at some point. He was absolutely a horrible human being, and he kicked my mom out of the house on Smith Road that her sister bought for her and left in her will. Now it was gone, contested in a will dispute. Mom was out just like that, because the court decided my aunt was not in her right mind when she gave the deed over to my mother. I assure you: she most definitely was. She had breast cancer, not a brain-eating amoeba.

This all went down during the same time that Scott and I were raising our little family of three children, with five pets, and an acre of land to tend to. As I've mentioned, I did everything around the house. Scott went to work and brought home the bacon, as they say. I did absolutely everything else for everyone, the story of my life.

When my mom was living with us, she used to call the girls to her room at 7 PM sharp to see what color dress Vanna White was wearing on *Wheel of Fortune*. They would guess, and the winner would get a little chocolate Hershey's Kiss. It was pretty adorable. The girls looked forward to running up and guessing the dress's color. My mother and Aunt Deane used to watch *Wheel of Fortune* and *Jeopardy* every single night, while on the phone together for an hour, five nights a week, for at least a decade when we were still on Smith Road. Sometimes, Deane would come over and watch in person, and it was so funny to see them so competitive with each other. The Wheel and Jeopardy nights continued long after Deane died. I would watch it with my mom. It meant a lot to her, then the kids.

Somehow, they found a way to bet on it for about $5 per question or puzzle. No one ever beat my mom at games that involved solving puzzles.

She was getting $200 checks quite often from those battles of wit with my aunt. I sometimes think that Deane did it to give my mom some joy. She had money to burn, and my mom didn't have much at all. Not until Emma came along was anyone as good at Tetris as my mom. It was crazy pants! *Tetris*, Scrabble, backgammon, *Wheel of Fortune*, *Jeopardy* and poker. She was a wicked poker player. Every year on her birthday, the family got together and played cards, ate Peanut M&M's, and some carry-out: pizza, Skyway, whatever. Every year on April 27th, for years after she died, we would host a poker party in her honor. We still get together and play now and again, and every single time, she comes up in the conversation. "Mom would have gone all in." "Mom would have bluffed on that hand." She is always there.

These memories of having my mom live with us while the kids were growing up are so bittersweet because they were, at their core, absolutely wonderful. At my core, I was resentful that my life was yet again being used to fuel hers, and we argued all the time. I could have handled it better. She could have, too.

The day she died, she said two things that I've never been able to unhear. The first was, "My poor little Tracey, someday you will be so sorry," insinuating that I'd been hard on her and would regret it, even though I don't believe in regret. She should have said, "My poor little Tracey, thank you so much for giving so much of your life, energy, and time so that my life would be better than it would have been without you."

She also said, "Please promise to take care of your sister. I worry about her so much." It was a very appropriate way to wrap up our time together, her life, to make me feel like it wasn't enough no matter what I gave up, including my shot at a more extensive musical career. Then she hit me with the possibility of a guilt-ridden life if I did not take care of my sister's well-being. "Please take care of your sister, I worry about her."

My mother's final words have never left my mind or heart. To be clear, I love my sister and she is more than self-sufficient. She doesn't need to be "looked after." She's got this. It's just better that she knows I've got her back, and I do. Words can't save us now.

My grown adult children have turned out to be wildly wonderful humans, partly due to the love they were surrounded by but mainly due to their own tenacity and intelligence. They all make music and are songwriters, singers, and musicians. Cory, a software engineer, made an amazing record with his band GodBrother. Cory and Mark Jendrisak Jr. (Son of Mark from Unit 5) are the only two permanent members of that band. Cory has two incredible daughters now, Mara and Iris, and they are my absolute joy.

Emma plays music with her band, Suitor. They are about to record their first studio project in Kansas with some hot indie producers that have taken a shine to them, as my Gram would have said. She's constantly popping into my head, that grandmother of mine. Emma is a full-time psychology student at Cleveland State University and should be wrapping that up soon. She is also a talented artist and writer, and I hope she will one day write and illustrate her own book. She's a very talented girl.

Marisa has a degree in Russian studies and has traveled extensively, including to Russia, Poland, and Germany. At this point, I can't even remember all the places she has been. She started hitting the world before the age of twenty. Like father, like daughter. She is an administrator at the Martin Scorsese Film School at New York University and lives in Brooklyn. Marisa also writes and records her own music.

I absolutely did have an unconventional way of raising and educating them. A typical high school education only works for some. I believe that people learn in different ways, at different speeds, and that needs to be individualized. I allowed them to switch to homeschooling now and again. I allowed them to leave the system early to get their GED because I felt it's just flogging a dead horse unless you are straight off to college, and they hadn't decided. It certainly caused a lot of negative attention from friends, family, and "powers that be." I stood my ground and believe they all exhibit above-normal intelligence and talent. They contribute to society and are quite well-rounded. Because they were allowed to escape the system and become educated with a say in their own future. I saw wisdom in that and opportunity, while some just saw me screwing it all up.

I have mentioned it already, and it's not a bad thing to me. I live my life in a certain way: I do what I want in the way that I see fit. This doesn't mean I totally disregard other people; it means that I march to a different drummer. That drummer, in my head, is Keith Moon. I plow through it, I direct it, I lead the charge. Never going to be a polished, refined, studied drummer like Stuart Copeland. I am all over the place. I respect Stuart Copeland very much, but sometimes I need to make a louder statement, which is what I did raising my brood. No regrets, Coyote.

WICKED STORM
Written by Tracey Thomas
From the 2020 album *My Roots Are Showing*

Sometimes we fail, sometimes twice,
You can't learn the lesson, if you're not listening,
And maybe the writings on the wall,
or maybe it's long since faded.
Maybe we lie to ourselves, to save our hearts.

This wicked storm, this wicked storm, it is finally passing,
Or maybe that's just the way I see it.
Watching it roll away, won't keep the dark at bay,
Better to close the window, and lock out your heart.
Better to close the window, and lock out your heart.

About Wicked Storm: *I wrote "Wicked Storm" after moving home from Madison, Ohio, and experiencing some emotional issues. When I get too in my head with anxiety, worry, and darkness, I can't write. My muse leaves (don't blame her), and I don't create.*

In this case, as I felt myself healing up from a year of bad decisions, I got my guitar out, and this song just created itself. It is a song, to me, that shows hope and healing. It also gives a stern warning to watch yourself because there is always another storm blowing through.

SIXTEEN: MY MUSIC FAMILY AND PASSING IT DOWN

What a long, twisted journey it has been. I have been on the same road for so long now that I'm often afraid to venture in a different direction. Maybe that is okay, or maybe it is limiting. Either way, it works for me. I am not as afraid of limits these days. I am unsure if I will ever quit, retire, or stop before I am forced to by some unseen force in the cosmos. I may, I may not.

I have retired from music so many times that I've lost track. Ryan Humbert may know. My dear friend, a brother from another mother. He is one of the only songwriting partners I have ever had, or more correctly, put up with. I am not usually fond of anyone's input into my brain, life, or songs, and yet here I am doing a memoir. He has produced albums for me and put me on stages I would not have stepped foot on otherwise.

I have often said he is responsible for the second wave of my career, the best of the waves I have surfed (I don't really surf; it just sounded poetic). I was still at home, raising children, doing my "Martha Stewart" thing. I love Martha despite her flawed delivery at times — I relate. Having wrapped up my punk rock days, and on hiatus from my solo career, Ryan found me and brought me back to the music scene, and I am forever grateful for that; it changed my course. I wasn't sure if it was something I wanted or needed, but it turned out to be both of those things.

Ryan told me he heard my song "Stand Alone" on the radio and reached out to the station to find out who the artist was because he quite liked it. We eventually met in person at a Catie Curtis show hosted by

The Summit FM (91.3 FM in Akron-Canton, a wonderful music-heavy public radio station), where he was volunteering. We hit it off, and that was that.

Ryan has been such a force for good in my life. He's hard-working to a fault, honest, and hell-bent on putting all his immense energy into whatever he takes on. We are both headstrong, and producing records for someone like me is probably not the easiest way to roll when you have your own mind and ideas about production. We both tend to put the shit next to the fan (rather than in front of it), and we have a shared, natural ability to do what it takes for the greater good. The greater good for both of us was always the records themselves.

Ryan is currently traveling the stratosphere with his band, The Shootouts, as they top the Americana radio charts, tour the country, perform regularly at the Grand Ole Opry in Nashville, and work with luminaries like Marty Stuart, Vince Gill, Rodney Crowell, and more. I have never known a harder-working person in this industry than Ryan Humbert. He is that very rare combination of management smarts and musical talent, and those roles co-exist in complete harmony within one body.

January 31, 2025, will be the release of the record I mentioned earlier. It will come out with this very book. *Words Can't Save Us Now* is an acoustic, poetic, moody singer/songwriter album. It was recorded at the incredible Son of Moondog Studios in Kent, owned by the wonderful Dave Sacchini. It also features some very talented friends backing me up, including The Shootouts members Brian Poston and Emily Bates, plus Bill Watson, Tim Longfellow, and Christine Petersilge. I firmly believe it's the best thing I have ever done as a writer and singer. I am thankful for everyone involved and endlessly appreciative that Ryan always finds the time to bring me back to the center. It's not lost on me.

Little Miss Akron

Great albums, in my opinion, have a couple of things in common, even if they aren't the same genre or similar musically. A well-crafted record shows the depth of thought and emotion; it's an energy that runs underneath, and we pick up on it as we listen. Of course, it's about the songs, the crafting, the mix, and—oh my God, don't skimp here—the mastering. It is also about the energy created by its creation if that makes sense. It does to me. My records and individual songs have emotional depth because they are experiential, based on moments in time that created that feeling. It becomes tangible. Some of them have a lighter vibe because I also know that pain can be overcome and joy is always on tap if you allow it.

I have had a few managers in my life; some are still sane, one is questionable. I have never, however, managed myself in any way, shape, or form, personally or professionally. I know when to fold 'em, as they say. I fold at anything that isn't just being the creator. I forget which side of the brain handles the numbers, math, systems, and formulas, but I don't have a lot going on on that side. The other side is overflowing with colors, melodies, ideas, and emotions. I should walk lopsided. I should limp, the weight of that side of my head should overwhelm the entirety of me. I should have one foot on the ground and the other floating up in the air a little bit, like a see-saw with one person on it.

I stay awake, thinking of lyrics and ideas to paint. I love to paint, but I am terrible. It doesn't mean I don't do it. I am obsessed with cooking and baking. I like both and don't lean more towards one or the other, like most food enthusiasts. I love anything that involves making something pretty and putting it on a plate. I hate to sew clothes, but I love working with fabric, so I make quilts for those people I adore.

I can't follow any directions. I must learn everything on my own, no matter what it is. I can't be taught in the way that most people can. I dive in and figure it out alone and uninstructed (a life theme). It was a very frustrating process for my parents, and I have heard that more than once, not only from them but from teachers as well. If you start instructing me, my brain shuts down. I will go into this weird zone that makes me feel sleepy, maybe? I remove myself and go on autopilot. I can't help it; I have tried and tried, and I still have no idea why I can't learn like others, but I cannot. I guess the best way to describe it is that I learn things by reverse engineering them. That is as close as I get to explaining my process.

For example, suppose I want to make a dish that I had in a restaurant, which happens all the damn time. In that case, I can't follow a recipe, so I have to pick it apart, note the flavors, textures, and smells, and then try putting it together without anything to read, like a cookbook. I can't do that. It turns into me doing a standing meditation while staring into space and floating in the Universe, all freeform and out there. I'm sure there is some diagnosis there; it's a learning disability, for sure. I don't know which one, but has it made that other side of my brain more active? Stronger? Mightier? I cook, I paint, I write songs, I sing songs, I love interior design, and I can put a room together on a twenty-buck bill. Okay, that part is an exaggeration, but it's close.

I once worked as a florist at Giant Eagle. Weird note: roses die when I touch them. They always have, and it's a problem. Scott used to buy me roses all the time. He is so sweet, always with the flowers. He recently did again and we just realized, after damn near 30 years of trying, that roses hate the shit out of me. They never bloom; they stay closed, droop, and die without ever realizing their potential, which is quite tragic. We've tried a couple of times to see if it was just me and my particular energy. If Scott was the only one who touched them, put them in the vase, and trimmed them, they were gorgeous, thrived, and fully opened. If I did, they withered and died. I finally just noted that I love a standard bouquet, like little wildflowers, something that isn't fancy or expensive. Pretty and simple. I have tried my entire life to garden. I love the idea of a flower and herb garden. Year after year, I buy the seeds and the plants, put them out, and they die. Last year, I planted some cherry tomatoes, and they actually lived. I was so excited. I ended up with four little tiny tomatoes! I brought them in, washed them, and gave them to Scott. I was so proud of myself. What a harvest that was, those four baby tomatoes.

It's very odd that there is a difference, but there most definitely is because indoor potted house plants love me. My house is full of lovely plants in pretty pots and they are wickedly happy with me and my peculiar energy. They find me fascinating, and they like it when I play music in the house, sing them songs, and dance like nobody's watching. My plants and dog know I have some mad dancing skills.

While I may toot my creative horn like Miles Davis, I don't even have a horn for my academic side. It's more like a recorder, one of those little plastic things they give you in sixth grade. Having said that, I do the best with what I have. Numbers throw me. Step-by-step instructions that require reading? Forget it. I am not into formulas, science, or math. All of it goes into a big void, a black hole, and then just gets absorbed by the cosmos. I'll sing you a song, cook you a meal, and paint you a terrible painting, but never ever have me do your taxes.

As I have said, I don't collaborate with people often when writing songs. I did while in Unit 5 with my forever brothers Bob, Mark, Augie, and Mike. I would come up with something musically, and I would lay the melody line down or write some lyrics. It's how I learned my craft, with those guys. Sometimes, they wrote songs and gave me an idea of the melody line, which is how we created together; it was a group effort. It taught me how to layer sounds and create melodies. I always heard the music in my head but couldn't get it out unless I just verbally hummed or sang the line of whatever instrument I heard. It wasn't always pretty, but it worked in a very basic way. It was the same with my band Persona 74. They brought a piece of music to the table and I blabbed melody and lyrics over it.

Eventually, I learned to play some guitar to get those parts out of my head and into a form where I could communicate. I have been lucky to have had some of the best people work on my solo projects. They would take my little guitar songs and arrange their parts, drums, guitar, bass, piano, whatever. They crafted their parts to round out my sound, and I am forever grateful to them.

John Gildersleeve was my guitarist friend and bandmate. He was brilliant and added so much that it made me look more important as a writer than I was. I miss him, as we have long since drifted apart. John Sferra, the amazing drummer of Glass Harp fame, also helped craft my early records.

Benjamin Payne, a local producer and musician, helped me create my album *My Roots Are Showing*, which is one of my favorite recordings of my career. We also started a band called The Crowders, which I believe was full of potential. I worked with his band Yankee Bravo on some things as well, and I appreciate his contribution to my journey during that era.

From a very early age, I fell in love with jazzy, sultry, smoky songs: the standards. Billie Holiday, Ella Fitzgerald, and Julie London were my favorites. I gravitated toward the female stylings of these songs. I always knew that one day, I wanted to put together a jazz act. I finally did with my old friend Tim Longfellow, one of the most brilliant musicians I have ever known.

Tim and I have worked together for two decades. He has played on my albums and is my partner in my jazz project. He is a friend, a co-creator, and someone I cherish. We recorded a live album called *Piano Bar*. It is a collection of our most requested songs, with special guests Brad Bolton playing guitar and mixing the whole record, and Terry Hynde of The Numbers Band 15-60-75 playing sax. It means a lot to me to have it to pass along to anyone who loves that music as much as I do.

Little Miss Akron

Tim is so popular in the Northeast Ohio (and beyond) music scene, he shines like the sun behind his piano. I am honored that he always finds time for me, and I adore him.

Though it is a life full of guys who create music, it is rounded out by some pretty special girlfriends. Jill Bacon Madden is owner of Jilly's Music Room in Akron, and keeper of my onstage career. We laugh, cry, drink wine, and sometimes share a menthol in the very haunted basement of the club. She has tucked me in, drunk as a skunk, let me cry, and has given me a job in her kitchen, where she, again, let me cry. We have a beautiful friendship, and I love her dearly.

My former cousin by marriage (still a friend), Susan Moodie, is a nurse, vegan, and political wolf. Mary Auerbach, retired teacher extraordinaire, is as obsessed with genealogy as I am and the mother of a bonafide rockstar. We've spent decades hanging out and laughing together, and I am grateful for them both.

Andrea Beckett is so prominent in this book and in my story. We met in middle school, had all of our rites of passage together, and she is the most like me of anyone I have ever known. We share a certain kind of crazy and are fabulous friends forever.

My sister-in-law Janelle Arnold is someone I cherish in my world. She is calm, together, not easily ruffled, and a great listener. I love her to the moon and back. Mark Jendrisak, my Unit 5 bandmate, will always hold a massive place in my heart as one of my best friends. We have laughed, cried, talked for hours, shared adventures, and seen each other married, divorced, married again, loved and lost, and more.

Melissa Ulrich, Linda Millar, Nancy Peters, and Amy Walker are my mates in The Crones and have become family to me. I love our time together, and I couldn't have picked a better bunch of bitches to spend my old lady days with.

These are my standouts, the people who are my clan, and we may fall in and out, but I know that I could call any of these people even after a decade, and if I needed them, there they would be. I am all about family first, but sometimes we need to have that extended branch of our tree, and these are my branches. I still count my sister Sandy (Sonny) as one of my closest friends.

When all is said and done, my very best friend is my husband, Scott, who is both family and bestie. We get each other. We share quality time together like I haven't ever had with anyone. I can be so unabashed about all my trials and tribulations, flaws, and quirks, and he is just there to balance it, accept it, and love me despite it all. We love music, good food, the ocean, and the mountains (I love the mountains more, and he loves the ocean more). We love each other's families, and we all just melted together in a significant way. We have shared over thirty years now, and sure, he drives me batshit crazy when he doesn't clean the kitchen counter after he makes something, or if he leaves his little balled-up napkins on the table, but I still look forward to him coming home after work.

I love going with Scott to Jilly's Music Room for a cocktail and a night out. I miss our yearly vacations, but record stores aren't what they once were, and yet he's still there, buried in decades of buying and collecting: vinyl, CDs, DVDs, all of it. It's a big sea of "stuff" that I can't break him away from. It brings him joy. We have enough to meet our simple needs, and we both appreciate the small things. We have had a lovely run of it and I am grateful. We have had a few fights in our decades together, but when I say a few, I mean it. Just a few. I would do it all again, but this time, I would tell him to sell the store before downloading music became a thing. Maybe we will do that next time and buy a little cottage with some land, let the kids run barefoot in the summer through the dog shit that is inevitable for this family. Run wild, step in all of it, and realize that it always washes off.

As I look back, reread this, take stuff out, and then put it back in, I realize I need to stop and leave it as it is. It has been nearly three years since I began writing, and I am forever changing it. If I don't just accept it and let it breathe, it will never be anything other than words on my computer. I am all at once afraid, overly judgemental of my work, and not wanting to share personal business while wanting to share it all. I feel like a walking contradiction, swinging wildly from one thing to the next and yet surprisingly not bipolar. I was tested for that one a couple of times actually, but nope, don't have that.

I guess when it's all said and done, I am proud of the life I have lived. I have overcome a lot, created a lot, and made a ton of mistakes that I have yet to learn from. I feel like it's been one big game of whack-a-mole since right out of the womb, so I'm genetically predisposed to whacking-the-mole. I try to keep my pretty flowers alive to no avail while singing songs with my cute white Gibson Dove knockoff guitar that I only bought because it is pretty.

Ultimately, I feel like the best way to explain myself to whoever comes after me, whether they contain this DNA of mine or not, is that I am a bit of a fairy trapped in the body of a human being. One that's a little put off by its limitations, truth be told. I am always and forever trying to fly above it all, getting knocked down and getting up again for another round. A phoenix from the ashes, that's me.

So here's to you—my children, grandchildren, and their children. Maybe one of you will own my guitar one day. That would be so cool.

Don't fuck it up.

EPILOGUE

Sometimes it is hard for me to believe that I was once crippled by panic attacks. After I gave birth to Emma, it was so bad that Scott would sit up with me all night. I could not leave the living room, so I slept on the sofa with Emma. Scott was right there with us, talking to me about how it would all pass soon once the meds started to work. He would sometimes play Mike Oldfield's music to relax me. After no sleep, he would get dressed in the morning and take newborn Emma to work, where he would tend to her during the day, then come home to sit with me all night again. This went on for three months.

I would sleep a little during the day once the sun came up. I was not eating and had lost quite a lot of weight. I remember Scott and my mom holding me and forcing torn bits of a banana into my mouth, holding my mouth closed so I would swallow.

I somehow managed to force myself to present a normal front for Cory. I would get him dressed, make him breakfast, and walk him to school, which was on the same block. I remember the pavement looking and feeling like it was buckling. I was so dizzy and afraid, but I did it every morning. Sometimes, on the way back to the house, I would end up sobbing and shaking, and then I would hit the couch and get a couple of hours of sleep. I have always dreaded the sunset. For some reason, it makes me feel anxious and depressed, sometimes in a very big way. Scott used to say, "Once the sun sets, you will feel better," and I did. I still do.

Prescription meds eventually helped my panic disorder/postpartum issues, and I was back to living my life. It amazes me today that I was ever in such a dark place. I went from being petrified of everything, especially being alone, to years later, taking a road trip to New York City to see my youngest daughter, Marisa, all by myself. On the way home, I stopped in Gettysburg, Pennsylvania, and stayed in a notoriously haunted bed and breakfast. I was the only guest in the six-bedroom inn directly across from a battlefield. I did have a few strange experiences there. Of note, I heard someone call my name, felt someone sit on the bed, and felt a man call me a "bitch" right into my ear. I stayed there alone all night. I didn't run from the spectre that was taunting me (though he never did show himself, the chickenshit).

The following morning, I had coffee alone on the battlefield as the sun rose. I was the only one around for as far as the eye could see. I walked and walked and said a prayer for all of the soldiers who had died beneath my feet. After spending the night in a place that tested my ability to understand anything I knew to be real, I was all alone. I was scared, but I dozed off even after I felt something sit on the bed next to me!

All it takes is a strong sense of self, knowing that you are more than the sum of your parts and physical experiences. I fight fear constantly, daily. Sometimes I win, sometimes I lose, but I am always willing to battle, even in Gettysburg, by myself.

You just never know what tomorrow, next week, or next year may bring, so you can't really focus on that. The reward is actually in the process, not in the outcome. The curtain closes, and the audience applauds.

SPACE ENOUGH
Written by Tracey Thomas & Ryan Humbert
From the 2012 album *Queen of Nothing*

I'm tired of running from my demons,
Into arms so tightly closed.
I'm trying harder than your seeing,
And I'm not sure why this is so.

Chorus
'Cause I don't need to be your Jesus,
Don't wanna be your Mary Magdalene.
All I need is space between us,
Space enough, to make my stand.

Desperation makes me ugly,
Resignation leaves me bound.
I can't be the one to save you,
But I'll hold on until I drown.

Bridge
Looking up is just like looking down,
But what you see is someone more profound.
Not sure if heaven gives off all that light,
But it ain't comin' from the ground.

Not hangin' on to this forever,
Probably winding down about now.
Restitution brings on it's own evil,
All I really want is to be found.
All I really want is to be found.

About Space Enough: *I wrote this song during a struggle in my marriage. Scott and I haven't struggled a lot, but we have a few times, just like everyone else. I was tired of not being "heard." That's my word, and I tend to overuse it. Sometimes, I feel like no one is hearing me. Scott was depressed after losing our house in Hudson; he went through a tough time. I didn't love the fallout, so I wrote this song.*

Scott is actually the one who came up with the idea of using Mary Magdalene in the song. I originally wrote, "I don't need to be your Jesus, don't want to be your Superman," but I didn't love it. Scott said, "What about Mary Magdalene?" BAM.

SPLINTER

Written by Tracey Thomas & Ryan Humbert
From the 2025 album *Words Can't Save Us Now*

I pulled a splinter from your hand,
And you fell apart like sinking sand,
You're tough in ways I can't understand,
But weak in ways that I had never planned.

Prechorus
You're full of brutal truths, and edges rough,
And I'm always saying way too much.

Chorus
So I'm damned if I do, and I'm damned if I don't
My choices are few and that's not good enough
The river keeps flowin' like I keep on knowin'
We're done, we're done, we're done.
We're done, we're done, we're done.

We talked for hours in your bed,
That tortured place you rest your head,
You had your fears, and I had my wine
But there was silence between the lines.

Prechorus
But I'm not here, to change your mind,
'Cause I don't want to waste my time.

Bridge
You spoke the truth, I took it hard,
An open wound right from the start,
But there's no need to count the tears,
Ain't no surprise endin' here.

About Splinter: *"Splinter" is about a relationship that isn't working anymore. It's that simple. The world is full of these songs, and maybe it doesn't say anything different, but I'm not sure it needs to. It simply needed to say what I needed to say. It's about being in a relationship and being so different, and being way over having to deal with the differences constructively. It's about being tired of not talking, not working on it, tired of trying to pound a square peg in a round hole. It's about calling it a day; life goes on, love goes on.*

"Splinter" is the first song on Words Can't Save Us Now and kicks off the album with some tape machine noise and studio banter. The album's guitars and vocals were recorded live to two-inch tape at Son of Moondog studios in Kent, Ohio, under the watchful eye of the amazing Dave Sacchini.

The first thing you hear is the tape machine getting up to speed, followed by guitarist extraordinaire Brian Poston setting the stage and counting us in. We left that chatter at the top of the record to set the mood and let the listener feel like they were right there in the studio with us.

HOPE FLIES

Written by Tracey Thomas & Ryan Humbert
From the 2012 album *Queen of Nothing*

Hope laid down in the back of the yard,
Looking for signs in the clouds she sees,
Jesus' face says he's coming for me,
Yeah, he's coming for me.
She's not ready, scared out of her mind,
But she will be steady when it comes her time,
Comes her time to fly.

Chorus
Hope flies, time bides,
Waiting for another sunrise.
Hope cries, as dreams die,
It's realized that now it's time for hope to fly.

Life goes on while she's looking for things,
Searching for things she may never find,
But it's been some years since love whispered in her ear.
And she's known some ghosts from a life before,
And she gets the most out of things she stored,
Stored away for years.

Bridge
Old war horses tell their stories,
Basking in their youthful glories,
Running to the stage for a curtain call,
That's already come and gone.

About Hope Flies: *"Hope Flies" is a song about growing older, thinking about how you want to wrap it up, and being afraid and ready simultaneously.*

In many ways, the Hope character is my mother; in other ways, she is me. My mother and I talked about this a lot: what it means to grow old, end up alone, or be afraid, and the fate of women who have raised their children, seen their husbands drift away, and found some hope in whatever "God" is.

As a child, I would lie in the grass and find images in the clouds. I loved it, and sometimes, I would fall asleep out there staring at the sky in my backyard. My mom often joined me and then would laugh about how hard it was to get back up.

It is about reflecting on the past, worrying about the future, and loving being something you are no longer worthy of because the years have tarnished you. "Hope Flies" is about accepting that the wheel keeps turning and that it's okay.

This song features amazing slide guitar work from Erin Vaughn, and a roaring Hammond organ solo from Tim Longfellow.

Traveler on the Wind
Written by Tracey Thomas
From the 1996 album *The Poet Tree*

If you see me, on the street here,
Somewhere in time, some other year, say hello.
Haven't I loved you sometime before?

Will you know me, under lamplight,
Under a moon glow in the night, whisper low.
Haven't you traveled way too far? Way too far.

Chorus
The traveler on the wind,
Doesn't know where life begins or where it ends, if it ends at all.
It's where the trees still grow and where clean water flows indefinite,
Indefinite and free.

When the wind blows, will you wonder,
Wander around through time and space, touch my face.
Haven't I touched you so long ago?

About Traveler on the Wind: *This is a song about time travel. I pictured myself in Dickens-era England, under a lamppost, waiting for my love from another lifetime to meet me there. I was very Wuthering Heights about the whole thing. It is about great loves coming back into our lives over and over again in different times and places. It's about reincarnation, magic, and connection.*

It was at first a story. I wanted to turn it into a book but needed more inspiration to go deep enough with the tale, so it became a song. I had a woman who was a fan of my music that had become seriously ill. Sadly, she passed away, home alone in her bed, and when they found her, this song was playing on repeat on her CD player. She used to tell me the line about life, "if it ends at all," gave her hope that maybe it doesn't.

THIS WORLD
Written by Tracey Thomas & Ryan Humbert
From the 2012 album *Queen of Nothing*

Oceans still rush their shores,
It started before you were born.
Moons rise, moons still fall,
You don't need to understand it all.

Prechorus
This world is very old,
This world is very old.

Chorus
Don't give up too soon,
Nothing matters more to me than you.
Don't stop your heart from beating,
Before, before it beats at all.

Dams break, and bridges rise,
People live, and people die.
Things change, and things remain the same.
No one ever, ever takes the blame.

Prechorus
This world is very small,
This world is very small.

About This World: *I wrote this song with Ryan after my son Cory struggled with his journey on this planet.*

He had such a rough start. I've spent a lifetime trying to ensure he found light at every turn despite all that darkness. As a mother, it was impossible, and I'm still unsure how we got out of it. As a family, it was very damaging knowing a member of our tribe was dealing with demons that wouldn't shut the hell up. I wanted so badly to tell him that life will always spit you out for a break every now and then.

It's a lot like childbirth. You suffer unbearably, and then you get a little break; it cycles on and on like that, and so does life. Ultimately, you have a baby, which brings spring, new beginnings, and new dawns to give you hope.

Cory found his place quite a while after it was written — not because of it, mind you, but he did. He's now thirty-six years old, with two children, clean and sober, and working as a successful software engineer. He is open about his struggles and is now a fantastic singer/songwriter in his own right. The album he created with his band GodBrother is fantastic. He writes lyrics that slay my soul and make me envious of his insight.

Because I had such a profound struggle after the suicide of his father, I didn't do very well when he started to exhibit the same patterns. I did what I always do: I took it to the page and wrote the lyrics to this song.

I remember having trouble getting through the recording, which is evident in my tone on the record. This is the one song that I cannot play live, and it pains me to even listen to it. I struggled with including it here, but it is essential to my story. I decided to share the lyrics and this story, with Cory's approval, because if anyone out there is struggling with thoughts of suicide, they need to know that they are not alone.

They also need to know that things can change in the blink of an eye. Light and dark, yin and yang, up and down we go. You can go from the ledge to dyeing Easter eggs with your children on a sunny afternoon, loving every sight, smell, and touch.

Don't hesitate to hesitate.

Note: If you or someone you know is at immediate risk, don't wait—call emergency services or the 988 phone hotline for immediate help.

Live at The Bank in Akron, Ohio, circa 1980

PHOTOS

Unit 5

Onstage with Unit 5, wearing my Wilma Flintstone pin

Unit 5 live at The Bank

Unit 5 live at The Akron Civic Theatre

Unit 5, from left to right: Bob Ethington, Tracey Thomas, Mike Johnson, Mark Jendrisak, and Paul 'Augie' Teagle

Unit 5 days, wearing my Bryan Ferry pin

Live at The Bank

Unit 5 promotional photo taken by my sister, Sandy

With Cory. Us against the world

With Cory. We both look like babies

Mr. & Mrs. Shepard, November 19, 1994

A night out with Scott

With Gram Hattie

Scott Shepard, the world's best dad

Cory and Tracey, all grown up

My beautiful daughters, Emma and Marisa

My sweet grandbabies, Mara and Iris

Marisa and Emma

My name in lights at the Akron Civic Theatre

The Creamettes promotional photo

Lights promotional photo

Queen of Nothing Promotional Photo

Photo by Eric Battershell

With Robert and Jack Kidney and Ryan Humbert

Andrea and Tracey, then...

...and forty-seven years later

With The Crones, live at the Rialto Theatre, Akron, Ohio

With Tim Longfellow

With Ryan Humbert

Photo by Thomas Apathy

LONG LIVE THE QUEEN

2012 Promotional Biography for *Queen of Nothing*
Written by Bill Gruber, Program Director of The Summit FM
in Akron, Ohio from 1986 to 2015

Moving to the Akron area circa 1985 as a student at Kent State University, I had already missed the first phase of Tracey Thomas's musical career, the years with bands Unit 5 and Gone to Egypt, dating back to her teenage days. After college and early in my career at radio station WAPS in Akron, I became aware of the voice and music of Tracey Thomas during her early tenure with the band Persona 74 in the 1990s.

The local Akron music scene then was ripe with musicians earnestly pursuing that era's alternative rock style and stardom, with low studio budgets and too much infatuation with bands like Depeche Mode. One day along comes some big old open reel tapes with nicely produced material, sung with heart, played with polish, and boasting lyrics of a more adult, reflective nature. The band was Persona 74, the vocalist was Tracey Thomas, and I was hooked.

One of these demos included a charming, handwritten note from Tracey, a note that could go down as the most self-deprecating, low-self-esteem missive in the history of music. For whatever reason, those lovely Persona 74 demos never saw the light of day as a finished album release. On many levels, perhaps sharing a band name with a brand of razor blades wasn't such a good idea.

Tracey went through some hellish personal moments during these years. Personal trauma has proven to be one of music's greatest muses. In Tracey's case, she channeled life's challenges—and later victories—into her solo debut album, the magnificent and often grandiose *Standing Alone*.

It was around this time I got to know Tracey as a person, not just a voice on record, only growing my respect and appreciation for who she is and what she does. For the first time in years, she began a regular live performance schedule, further cementing my appreciation.

Standing Alone was followed by the more acoustic and restrained *The Poet Tree* album. With this album, Tracey seemed to gain the self-confidence worthy of her musical and lyrical accomplishments. Around this time, I humorously confronted Tracey with that rambling note she had written almost a decade earlier, asking her what advice she could pass on to the insecure young singer-songwriter who penned it.

As she began reading her handwritten own words from what seemed a lifetime ago, her eyes widened, and she began repeating, "On my god, this was me, this was me!" At that moment, it was obvious that Tracey Thomas had arrived, both professionally and personally. While fame and fortune officially eluded her, Tracey was at peace with herself, her life, her family, and her friends.

In recent years, Tracey has continued to release albums when the time felt right, whether the glossy and ambitious *Lights* (2001), the stripped-down and rootsy *Dancing In Cairo* (2003), or the confident and genuine *Ghost Town* (2007). Tracey has performed locally in the corner of her husband's Time Traveler record store, in dozens of smoky music venues that have mostly come and gone, to the 2,500-seat majesty of the historic Akron Civic Theatre, as well as traveling to "Big Apple" showcases at Danceteria and CBGB. Tracey has shared the stage with six decades of musical greats, ranging from pop traditionalists like Judy Collins and Melanie to rocked-out moments with punk/new wave legends Tin Huey, Black Flag, and The Dead Boys, to the twenty-first century blues-rock phenomenon, The Black Keys.

It is 2012 now; time for both the next phase of the recorded life of Tracey Thomas, her *Queen of Nothing* album of all new material, and the first-ever "best of" collection of her recorded material going back to Unit 5 days and covering over thirty years of her career.

If this is all new to you, welcome to the music of Tracey Thomas. Spend some time and hear what you've been missing. If Tracey Thomas has been a part of your life, congratulations and welcome to the latest chapter in the words and music of Tracey Thomas, the "Queen of Nothing."

TRACEY THOMAS DISCOGRAPHY

All songs written by Tracey Thomas unless otherwise noted.

Thank you to all the musicians, co-writers, engineers, producers, and everyone involved in the making of these albums.

www.traceythomasmusic.com

Unit 5
45 RPM
Sharkskin Records • 1981

Produced by Nick Nicholis & Unit 5

Side A
Decisions *(Ethington)*

Side B
Gracefully and Ladylike *(Johnson/Thomas)*

Unit 5
Scared of the Dark
Clone Records • 1981

Produced by Nick Nicholis & Unit 5

Side A
1. No Ones Girl *(Johnson)*
2. Big Kids *(Johnson/Ethington)*
3. Mental State *(Jendrisak)*
4. Ready *(Jendrasik/Thomas)*
5. Decisions *(Ethington)*
6. Like Lovers Feel *(Ethington)*

Side B
1. Go Ahead and Kiss Her *(Johnson)*
2. Fickle Hearts *(Ethington)*
3. Gracefully and Lady Like *(Johnson/Thomas)*
4. Lucky Charms *(Jendrisak/Johnson/Thomas)*
5. Believe It *(Jendrisak)*
6. Scared of the Dark *(Ethington)*

Tracey Thomas
Standing Alone
Relevart Records • 1993

**Produced by
Tracey Thomas & Freddie Salem
Executive Producer: Scott Shepard**

1. Stand Alone *(Thomas/Henterley)*
2. Lightning *(Thomas/Kidd/Anders/Lee)*
3. Wicked *(Thomas/Henterley/Henterley)*
4. Switch in the Dark *(Thomas/Anders)*
5. Right Words *(Thomas/Henterley/Henterley/Kidd)*
6. I Can See It Now *(Ethington)*
7. She Comes in Colors *(Lee)*
8. Blow Away *(Thomas/Henterley/Henterley/Kidd)*
9. Web of Silence *(Thomas/Henterley/Henterley/Kidd)*
10. Lay Down *(Feat. Jane Aire) (Safka)*
11. Stand Alone *(Acoustic) (Thomas/Henterley)*

Tracey Thomas
The Poet Tree
Relevart Records • 1996

**Produced by
Scott Shepard & Tracey Thomas**

1. Yesterday's Child
2. It Doesn't Matter
3. Traveler on the Wind
4. I Thought You Knew It
5. Secrets in the Attic
6. Blind
7. Water
8. Here I Go Again
9. You Don't Argue
10. Silent Erosion
11. Forgiving

About The Poet Tree: *I had always wanted to make a folk album. I grew up listening to folk music and learned to sing with Peter, Paul and Mary, one of my sister's favorite acts. I got caught up being a punk rocker. I remember coming up with the album title and thinking it was pretty clever. So, I began to craft some of my poems into songs.*

The album, in its entirety, was written during a bad bit of Postpartum depression. It's not a cheerful album; it's full of sadness but also a little bit of hope. Of all the albums I have written that were hideously personal, this comes second only to Words Can't Save Us Now.

Tracey Thomas
Lights
Relevart Records • 2000

Produced by Dave Stephenson
Executive Producers:
Tracey Thomas & Scott Shepard

1. Four Seasons
2. Change Your World *(Thomas / Stephenson)*
3. Strange Bedfellows
4. Grace
5. Easter *(Hogarth)*
6. You Don't Love Anymore *(Thomas / Stephenson)*
7. The Forest
8. Divine Intervention
9. What Else is New
10. Pleasure and Pain

About Lights: *Lights was a collection of songs that needed a place to live. So, I took to the studio to create. I had a piece of a song; it was meant to be finished, but it ended up being just a little intro. Once I heard it, I felt like that was its sole purpose, so I opened the record with it as a lead-in to "Four Seasons" and made it the title track. I love doing little bits of things like that that can stand on their own, knowing they don't need to evolve because they are perfect the way they are. I also did that with a song called "Lavender" on My Roots Are Showing.*

Lights found me working with guitarist John Gildersleeve. John and I worked together for many years, and I will always be so appreciative of his David Gilmour-like presence on my records. I always found his work on this record and at live shows to be stellar. One of my favorite songs we recorded together is "Change Your World." Of all my albums, if I could go into the studio and do "Tracey's version" today with new technology and more experience, Lights would be the one I would take on.

Tracey Thomas
Dancing in Cairo
Relevart Records • 2003

**Produced by
Tracey Thomas & Ryan Humbert
Executive Producer: Scott Shepard**

1. Melancholy Moon *(Thomas/Humbert)*
2. Brokendown
3. This Time Around
4. Follow You Down *(Thomas/Humbert)*
5. Night Vagabonds
6. Same to Me
7. I Know Better
8. You Go Your Way *(Thomas/Humbert)*
9. Everything
10. Melancholy Moon *(Reprise) (Thomas/Humbert)*

About Dancing in Cairo: *Dancing in Cairo was not pre-conceived; there was no "concept" planned for this album. Sometimes, my albums are just a collection of songs that started to pile up, and I hit the studio with them. Others have more of a concept, for example, My Roots Are Showing and Words Can't Save Us Now.*

The album ended up with a bit of a "country" sound due to the fiddle and mandolin skills of Jeff Snauffer, who tragically passed away at the age of thirty, just four months after we made this album.

My co-producer Ryan Humbert devised the idea to record it live in an old historical one-room church in a tiny unincorporated part of Plain Township called Cairo, Ohio, near North Canton. I had no album title, just some songs to mess with. During the sessions, I literally danced around listening to some tracks. I started mumbling, "I'm dancing in Cairo." And, it stuck.

Tracey Thomas
Ghost Town
Relevart Records • 2007

Produced by Ryan Humbert

1. Ghost Town
2. Running Away
3. All Roads Lead to You
4. Incognito *(Thomas/Humbert)*
5. Before Me
6. Like Water Runs
7. Someday *(Thomas/Humbert)*
8. Ain't I a Woman
9. Rabbit Hole *(Thomas/Humbert)*
10. Telescope *(Thomas/Humbert)*
11. Sing Me Home *(Thomas/Humbert)*
12. Dancing in the Dark *(Springsteen)*

Tracey Thomas
Queen of Nothing
Relevart Records • 2012

Produced by Ryan Humbert

1. Queen of Nothing
2. Hope Flies *(Thomas/Humbert)*
3. Better Than Anyone *(Thomas/Humbert)*
4. Blue Eyes *(Thomas/Humbert)*
5. Falling Down *(Thomas/Humbert)*
6. This World *(Thomas/Humbert)*
7. Hey, Save Me *(Thomas/Humbert)*
8. Blind & Faithful *(Thomas/Humbert)*
9. Weathering the Storm *(Thomas/Humbert)*
10. Every Little Time *(Humbert)*
11. Space Enough *(Thomas/Humbert)*

About Queen of Nothing: *This album started as a collection of songs about retiring. I was hell-bent on "getting out of the biz." I felt too old, and it seemed like I was aging out of my career (unpleasant). I also had a long period of writer's block. I decided to present the bits and pieces of songs I had started to Ryan to see if we could turn them into something.*

We sat down at my home in Hudson with pages of lyrics, a few guitars, and my dogs. I played what I had, and the spark was lit. We immediately hit a stride and wrote the better part of five songs in one day. Ryan did his thing by adding more chords and structure to keep me from being redundant.

After that, the rest flowed out and created itself, as will happen sometimes. Life is what happens when you are making other plans. Same with records, I guess.

Tracey Thomas
Ghosts in the Woodwork:
The Best of Tracey Thomas
Relevart Records • 2012

Compilation Produced
by Ryan Humbert

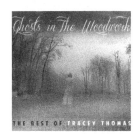

1. Go Ahead and Kiss Her *(w/ Unit 5) (Johnson)*
2. Stand Alone *(Thomas/Henterley)*
3. Web of Silence *(Thomas/Henterley/Henterley/Kidd)*
4. Switch in the Dark *(Thomas/Anders)*
5. Blow Away *(Thomas/Henterley/Henterley/Kidd)*
6. Yesterday's Child
7. Water
8. Strange Bedfellows *(Single Edit)*
9. Divine Intervention
10. Night Vagabonds
11. Follow You Down *(Thomas/Humbert)*
12. Running Away
13. Ain't I a Woman
14. Someday *(Thomas/Humbert)*
15. Incognito *(Thomas/Humbert)*
16. Before Me
17. Blue Eyes *(Thomas/Humbert)*
18. Queen of Nothing
19. Better Than Anyone *(Thomas/Humbert)*

Bonus Tracks:
20. Brokendown *(2012 Version)*
21. God Bless The Child *(Holiday/Herzog Jr.)*
22. Stand Alone *(Acoustic) (Thomas/Henterley)*

Tracey Thomas
Fine & Mellow:
The Music of Billie Holiday
2013

Recorded live at the
Akron Civic Theatre
Akron, Ohio

An official live bootleg featuring songs recorded by Billie Holiday:

1. Gloomy Sunday *(Seress)*
2. More Than You Know *(Rose/Eliscu/Youmans)*
3. When a Woman Loves a Man *(Mercer/Hanighen/Jenkins)*
4. Good Morning Heartache *(Higginbotham/Drake/Fisher)*
5. Ain't Nobody's Business *(Grainger/Everett)*
6. Summertime *(Gershwin/Heyward/Gershwin)*
7. Body and Soul *(Heyman/Sour/Eyton)*
8. Fine and Mellow *(Holiday)*
9. Act Two Intro
10. Don't Explain *(Holiday/Herzog Jr.)*
11. In My Solitude *(Ellington/DeLange/Mills)*
12. Lover Man *(Sherman/Davis/Ramirez)*
13. Billie's Blues *(Holiday)*
14. Some Other Spring *(Herzog Jr./Kitchings)*
15. Stormy Weather *(Koehler)*
16. God Bless The Child *(Holiday/Herzog Jr.)*
17. My Man *(Willemetz/Pollock/Charles/Yvain)*
18. Strange Fruit *(Meeropol)*
19. Lady Sings the Blues *(Holiday/Nichols)*

Tracey Thomas
My Roots Are Showing
Relevart Records • 2020

Produced by
Tracey Thomas & Benjamin Payne

1. Lavendar
2. Float Away
3. It's Usually Love
4. Cold
5. Restless Devil
6. The Crush
7. Wicked Storm
8. Growing Weary
9. Out From Under
10. Would You Cry?
11. Sorry Mister
12. Oh, Virginia

About My Roots Are Showing: *My Roots Are Showing is my musical autobiography. Each song connects to how I think, act, live, and love. It pays tribute to my roots, quite literally, and to my family and ancestors. It digs into this Appalachian soul of mine and embraces the magic of my people and their love for the mountains, in particular Virginia. It's the music I sit and play on the front porch with a bourbon as the sun sets or on the back deck with coffee as the sun rises. It takes me back to our home in Hudson where I did both of those things. One lane road, dead end street, an acre of land with fields and a swamp in the back, unencumbered by humans. Out front, nothing but trails in the National Park system. I listened to crickets and baby frogs in the spring. I'll never forget it. The idea for this album started then, but it took another four years to come to fruition. I worked on it with trusted friends and again recorded it in an old church in Seville, Ohio, under the watchful eye of Benjamin Payne. I am all over this one: production, writing, guitar, vocals, and album art. I love this album; it's deeply personal, and I am really proud of it.*

Tracey Thomas & Tim Longfellow
Piano Bar
2023

Featuring
Brad Bolton & Terry Hynde
Recorded live at
Jilly's Music Room
Akron, Ohio

1. Summertime *(Gershwin/Heyward/Gershwin)*
2. At Last *(Warren/Gordon)*
3. Stormy Weather *(Koehler)*
4. Good Morning Heartache *(Drake)*
5. Cry Me a River *(Hamilton)*
6. Someone to Watch Over Me *(Gershwin/Dietz/Gershwin)*
7. Fine & Mellow *(Holiday)*
8. Lover Man *(Sherman/Davis/Ramirez)*
9. My Funny Valentine *(Hart)*

Tracey Thomas
Words Can't Save Us Now
Relevart Records • 2025

Produced by Ryan Humbert
Additional Production by
Brian Poston & Tracey Thomas

Side A
1. Splinter *(Thomas/Humbert)*
2. Wax on Fire *(Thomas/Humbert)*
3. The Whole of the Moon *(Scott)*
4. Fade to Black *(Thomas/Humbert)*
5. Every Breaking Wave *(Evans/Hewson)*

Side B
1. This is Me Trying *(Swift)*
2. Words Can't Save Us Now *(Thomas/Humbert)*
3. So It Goes *(Thomas/Humbert)*
4. Follow The Moon *(Ballard)*

BONUS TRACK
(Unedited)
By Robert Kidney

A note from Tracey: *When I sat down to pen my memoir, I wanted my friend Robert Kidney of The Numbers Band 15-60-75 to write the intro. He uses words to create images unlike anyone I have ever known. I thought it would be an interesting take on, well, me as seen through his eyes. I assumed he would write a couple of short paragraphs about his good friend...me. Little did I know he would write an entirely independent story, in Robert's speak, with words tumbling about, creating abstract art and moody visuals. I should have expected that because he's not the kind of guy who would just say, "My friend Tracey is cool." So here's to my one-of-a-kind friend, artist, musician, and painter Robert Kidney, who now has a "bonus track" in my book to close it out. It will go to print completely unedited, undisciplined, and very much a chapter unto itself. Per his instructions, "No fucking editor is going to change my piece." So, none of the animals in this production have been harmed.*

So, you've been sitting here waiting in the coffee shop nursing your latte. She's fifteen-twenty minutes late as usual, comes bursting through the door, sees you with eyes that throw her usual bouquet of flowers disappearing as they separate flying past your eyes. She sits down, smiles, and gives you a book, looks down for a moment, looks up, I'm sorry my watch is upside down and begins to tell you this is the story of my life, how every life is a story full of hard edges and rage, futility the possibility of love, an understanding hopefully of happiness contentment peace of mind quiet, always challenged by the unforeseen should have seen, tragedy loss irretrievable error and the potential to become triumphant. Every life is important; every story should be told; this is the only one I know.

A story of hard-cracked concrete sidewalks grown in weeds, hot sun, black asphalt streets turn to bleak night rain that soaks as if it would never stop running deep in the gutters to rooms where bare light bulbs ache despair, stark desperate fear, longing left forever in a lost child speaks no words, doesn't understand, trapped in a prison called home, a full house of ignorance, alcoholism uncontrolled, unpredictable, unpreventable violence a wasteland, of abandonment loveless isolation emotional collapse and instability, leaves unrepairable damage grow in too many fleeting dim lit dread filled ransacked houses of broken cupboards smashed crockery thrown against the wall next to a table fists pound upon enraged, spits drunken ashtray vinegar breath his terror-filled poisonous threat.

Soft childhood footsteps through new rain in spring grass lead to a path through shadowed woods dissolve in a parking lot, and a back seat bedroom of belongings stuffed in the trunk will end up coming down the kitty-catwalk child model meets her first encounter with innocent attention acceptance and affection of complete strangers, the foundation of stage performance and entertainment. At that moment, the search began to attain this attention through some yet undiscovered ability unknowingly through what would become persistence and a desire that led to footsteps on a pathway down a runway to a hallway of abuse from hungover, insensitive, resentment-filled teachers and snotty brats who grew up to become snot brat hungover insensitive resentment filled bosses. But with hardheaded determination, tough-skinned tolerance, and curiosity beyond her vulnerability gains forever friends, first loves, lifelong close ties, but most importantly, the discovery of and battle with insecurity and self-esteem that unveiled a lasting love for the performance of music and the discovery of the Angel within her whose voice became her voice, and gave her a reason and a direction an everlasting desire to be part of the soul of music, in spite of all the tangled vine thickets it's surrounded by. Got the wrong man in the wrong marriage, alcoholic, drug addicted, eventually a revolver is being pointed at her first baby in her arms, wielded by a lost on a long ride down some broken road man led to suicide. Took the twenty lane highway to Hollywood that ends in Lost Vegas that becomes some two lane runnin through Tuscaloosa back seeking artistic acceptance, just to get fame thrower blowtorched by the organ grinders feedin long pig to egos of fake music carnies, carnalvores devouring the hyped-up sexy music scene back home in Bleakville. The imaginary distorted self-induced highly inflated bitterly opinionated greed for success center of the universe, that tried to kill her, but failed miserably as it crashed and burned she walks out through the debris with indelible memories good and bad genuine relationships good and bad friends artists musicians, most importantly a more precise perspective. What she wants and wants to become who she is, and who she will refuse to become when shoved fed up against the fence of the next dead end, this time broke away in a rage busts open the fire exit door into a another dark theatre grasping stumbling falling stands back up in the aisle unrestrained shoving past it all just to finally reach some light to be free out on the street again just to have an opportunity to begin another again, this time with courage reassured tenacity that defines then defends a deep embracing all-encompassing ability to love, defiantly left untouched in her steep climb to slammed doors.

Wanders hospital hallways into rooms filled with the trauma of loved ones tragic beyond tears rooms of her own dire confusion unrelenting hopelessness, must somehow find determination persevere never relinquish live, spite it all. The hard deep exhausting work of the care for others and self-realization required to overcome fear despite the churning phantom of an unknown future. Rebirth against early death called recovery, childbirth in the face of death. The conundrum of unforgiven love left by abuse collides with the inability to forgive becomes overwhelmed by forgiveness.

As always her life's blood of memory forever returns on dusty worn out summer roads to Appalachia, born with its mystic veil superstitions language the charmed beauty insistent severity of ignorance tempered by outrageous humor, stories of complex characters in her family how their history of beliefs effect her spirit, other empty distant roads run deeper south to magic shape shifting ancient secrets born in prehistory. Cracker Jack O'Cult forays evolve into an awareness of synchronicity and clairvoyance reveal the unshakeable belief in the something infinitely more important than what we call existence, understanding that when opened, these various antique doors provoke consideration as to where they open to without and within, that which owns and troubles us.

Leaving an irrepressible openness not naive cultivated, allows the chance discovery of someone who loves her as she is, that loves her life as it is, and persists to make it whole, softer, this love so rare. Begins living in the events of endless love, her children a husband and how it breaks and how to keep it safe though it breaks, bringing to this challenge the strength and weight of a life survived, which almost imperceivably began to redeem then reconcile a return to her original artistic dream, a dream set aside the dream she continues to follow as I write this and wish her well, knowing this hard edged wonder that is always life will continue challenge her life, test its strength as she endures and triumphs.